Navigating Your
Federal Retirement

Your Successful Passage into Financial Freedom

BRANDON CHRISTY CPA, PFS

For more information contact:
Brandon S. Christy, CPA, PFS
Retirement Benefits Institute, Inc.
2939 McManus Road
Macon GA, 31220
(877) - 864 - 1145

978-0-692-47436-5 - paperback
978-0-692-47435-8 - eBook

Library of Congress Control Number: 2015939617

To Cara, Seth, Callie, Joseph, and Connor.
Thank you, Lord, for such a wonderful family.

CONTENTS

RBI: Helping You Navigate Your Retirement

ONE THING HAS become abundantly clear to me in my more than six years of helping federal employees plan for retirement and manage their assets: you cannot plan for retirement successfully if you don't know and understand all of your options.

Before we get started, I would like to clarify some viewpoints you will see throughout the reading of this book. I am, by trade, a Certified Public Accountant as well as a Personal Financial Specialist. In the length of my career, I also became the President of two businesses—Retirement Benefits Institute (an educational training company and publisher of this book) and Christy Capital Management (a financial planning firm), and I apply all three roles to the concepts addressed in this book. The stories found in this book involve realistic situations which are familiar as individuals plan for a sound retirement.

The retirement options available to federal employees are numerous and complex. Multiple federal retirement systems with many special rules and provisions are available. As a federal employee, your benefits package is made up of many parts that interact with one another, often in surprising ways. Planning for retirement requires a holistic view of all of your benefits, your finances, your needs, your lifestyle, and your budget. You must make several decisions that will have permanent consequences for your future. The decisions you make now can determine your financial security during retirement.

For more than five years, Retirement Benefits Institute has been helping federal employees realize that dream. We conduct focused training sessions to help federal employees understand the intricacies of their retirement package, and to help them choose the benefits that best fit into their overall retirement picture.

Federal employees must understand and use all of the programs and options available to them to construct a healthy and sustainable retirement income. Although pensions still exist in the public sector, budget constraints have forced most government employers to reduce employee pensions. Few government employees working today will receive a pension sufficient to cover all of their retirement expenses unless they scale back their lifestyles significantly. Most private-sector employees today contribute to and draw upon Social Security and put aside substantial funds in retirement savings plans such as TSPs, IRAs, 401(k)s, and other retirement accounts.

Unfortunately, federal employees often don't pay adequate attention to retirement planning. Everyone intends to stay on top of his or her retirement planning, but life tends to get in the way. Busy people put off making decisions about retirement, often until it is too late to take advantage of all their best options. Working professionals may have trouble finding the time to really understand their retirement package. This is a costly mistake you do not want to make. If you do not fully understand your benefits package, you are most likely leaving money on the table.

GETTING THE HELP YOU NEED

All government benefits programs have free program specialists who can explain, usually over the phone, the intricacies of these particular programs. Take advantage of these resources, but also find someone who can advise you about the system as a whole and demonstrate how the various programs will fit with your individual finances and life in retirement. It isn't enough to memorize pamphlets from the federal government's Office of Personnel Management (OPM) website (opm.gov). OPM will give you a snapshot of only one segment of your retirement picture—an important perspective, but still only one. You also need to understand how your federal pension will interact with your other retirement income, including your savings accounts and, if you are eligible, Social Security. You have to understand how taxes, various tax-advantaged savings plans, health care costs, inflation, and other factors will affect your benefits and personal finances in retirement.

As a federal employee, your options as you move toward retirement are different from those of private-sector employees. If your advisor is versed only in traditional personal savings vehicles such as 401(k)s and IRAs, they may not know enough about FERS, CSRS, TSP, or other federal employee options to give you complete or fully accurate financial advice. As a federal government retiree, it is imperative that you and your advisors understand all of the complexities of your benefits package and how it fits into your greater financial picture.

Retirement Benefits Institute places a heavy emphasis on education for all these reasons we've mentioned. We provide federal employees with the information they need to make the right decisions about retirement. We do this because we believe that only you can make decisions about your retirement.

Because we focus specifically on federal employees, we have an intimate knowledge of most aspects of the many federal benefits programs, and we understand the challenges faced by federal government retirees. The subsequent chapters will provide comprehensive information about the many components of the various federal benefits packages, and they will help you to successfully integrate these benefits with your life goals and your legacy planning. This book will also offer a glimpse into the lives of federal employees. We hope that you can learn from their mistakes and successes so that your retirement proceeds with as few hiccups as possible.

While this book mirrors Retirement Benefits Institute's training program, one is not a substitute for the other. Let this book serve as an introduction to the concepts discussed in that program and be a reference you can use throughout your working life and retirement. We hope this book allows us to reach more people, but it is only the beginning of the conversation. Ultimately, the goal of this book is to educate you and compel you to take an active role in your retirement planning.

PLANNING FOR TOMORROW TODAY

What separates the success stories from the tragic failures in financial planning is, as the term implies, sound *planning*. This may seem obvious, but many federal employees fail to start thinking about retirement until it is just around the corner. Earlier is better, but whatever your age, career stage, or retirement goals, the time to start planning is always now.

This book is a direct call to action. If you are a federal employee approaching retirement, you need to take control of your financial future before it is too late. Opportunities to maximize your retirement income may be passing you by. For example, the earlier you start saving, the more you can put in your TSP and other retirement accounts. These tax-advantaged accounts have yearly contribution limits, which means the sooner you start saving, the more assets you can shelter (and the longer your assets may be able to grow tax-free).

Are you on the verge of retirement and not sure what it will look like? It's not too late to get started on the right path, or to change your course.

THE RETIREMENT NOBODY WANTS

Consider the case of Jim, a retiree who came to us for assistance. Jim had decided that he would retire from the federal government the day he turned sixty years old. He had been desperate to leave the workforce so that he and his wife, Katherine, could really start enjoying life. He had resolved to retire at sixty no matter what his financial situation was. By the time his sixtieth birthday rolled around, he had already submitted his retirement notice. He was ready to bid his coworkers good-bye and then—*finally*—set about the business of retirement planning.

He started filling out all the paperwork without first seeing a financial professional who was well-versed in federal benefits, and in the course of this process, he opted to leave his wife a full survivor benefit at his death without understanding the repercussions—good *and bad*—of choosing that option. Leaving his spouse a full benefit seemed like the only reasonable option.

What Jim didn't realize was how this choice would affect his retirement income. This decision subsequently cost Jim 10 percent of his annuity, which came as a shock! He had been counting on that monthly $400 so he and his wife could travel, as they had planned when they were younger. Jim couldn't believe that one simple choice could cost him 10 percent of his annuity. He was outraged, but there was little he could do—he had chosen unwisely. His choice was an understandable retirement income planning mistake—but a mistake nonetheless, and one that would cost Jim and his wife for many years to come.

Because Jim was only sixty, he was not yet eligible to start drawing from Social Security. His pension was also lower than he had expected. This left only his personal savings fully intact. To make up the retirement income deficit, Jim started spending from his Thrift Savings Plan (TSP—a tax-advantaged personal savings account for federal employees) and other savings accounts almost immediately upon retirement.

This situation became doubly problematic when a sudden market downturn halved his savings almost overnight! Although Jim knew the market would eventually recover, he had no other option but to draw on his savings now—and every dollar he spent during the downturn was like spending two dollars he had saved! The market did recover eventually, but Jim and Katherine did not. They had spent too much of their savings before the markets recovered, and they continued to struggle throughout retirement. Because Jim's TSP was so depleted, he was forced to take Social Security as soon as he was eligible at age sixty-two, even though this meant a reduction in his benefit. Despite this penalty, he had no choice—they needed the income immediately.

Even with the added income from his Social Security check, Jim still ended up spending most of his TSP during his sixties. This situation occurred partly because he had depleted his TSP earlier, and partly because he never got a handle on how to budget his expenses. He often provided financial support to his adult children whenever they needed it, which caused further money struggles.

Tragedy struck again when Katherine was diagnosed with cancer. Though she received aggressive, expensive treatments, the cancer still metastasized and she passed away at age seventy. This was not only a personal tragedy, but also a financial one. Since retiring, Jim had paid more than $35,000 in survivor benefits for his wife that could never be recovered; she had passed away before receiving the survivor benefits. In addition to the emotional pain of losing his wife, Jim was much worse off financially without her. He was no longer receiving her Social Security check because it had been the smaller of the two. He has now moved from the "married filing jointly" tax bracket to the single tax bracket—thus suffering a higher marginal tax burden. He was left with his pension, his one Social Security check, and practically no TSP funds remaining. The only redeeming detail was that Jim was now receiving his full pension without the 10 percent reduction for survivor benefits. But severe damage had already been done: Without enough in TSP savings to produce substantial returns, Jim was barely able to make ends meet throughout his seventies.

Worse, Jim and Katherine never got to travel as they had wanted. They were never able to enjoy the retirement lifestyle they had spent their whole lives working toward. This was twice a tragedy—the first tragedy being so many dashed dreams, and the second being that so much of it could have been avoided. If only Jim had waited a few more years to retire, chosen not to draw Social Security so early, better protected his TSP funds, and made smarter budgeting decisions, he and Katherine would have been better positioned to enjoy happy years savoring the luxurious retirement for which they had worked all their lives.

I share Jim and Katherine's story not to scare you, but as a call to action. Your story doesn't have to turn out this way. You don't need to have started planning from the age of eighteen or twenty-two, but you must start maximizing your retirement income now. Plenty of success stories are out there, even among people who waited longer than they should have to start planning for retirement.

A LITTLE PLANNING GOES A LONG WAY

Consider the case of Robert and Sharon. I first met Robert and Sharon five years ago when they attended one of our federal benefits training events. As an air traffic controller, Robert would face mandatory retirement at age fifty-six. He understood that retiring at such an early age would create special challenges for his retirement finances, but he resolved to get ahead of potential problems by learning everything he could about his options beforehand and crafting a plan. He came to our training session for just this reason.

After the seminar when Robert and Sharon reviewed their personal finances, things didn't look very promising. They had substantial expenses, largely because they had a lot of debt— credit card debt, a car loan, and a mortgage they would be paying into retirement. They also had one child who would soon be going to college. At first glance, it was hard to see how they could reduce their debt and find a way to build a comfortable retirement income before Robert was forced to retire.

Robert and Sharon didn't have a lot of things going for them, but they had done one important thing correctly: they hadn't waited until retirement to *start* planning for their future.

The first thing they did was tackle their massive debt by paying down the debt aggressively. Setting a stringent but reasonable budget helped them whittle their credit card debt down to zero, pay off their car, and still pay for their son's college education.

Despite their progress, the house note was still looming. Robert requested a one-year extension for his retirement, and miraculously he was granted this opportunity. He now had an additional two years to get his finances in order. With all of their other debts paid down, the couple was able to concentrate on paying down the mortgage so they could enter retirement with no debt load, which they did.

Robert and Sharon had to work hard and make some sacrifices, but their efforts paid off handsomely, and life looks pretty good for them now. As of this writing, they are working on a $70,000 remodeling project that will transform their house into the retirement dream home they have always wanted.

Make no mistake: getting Robert and Sharon to this point took lots of planning. Paying off their debt was just the first step; they still had to formulate a plan that would provide them a good income in retirement. Because Robert was younger than fifty-nine and a half when he retired, he would be subject to a 10 percent early withdrawal penalty on his IRAs. They decided to leave enough in his TSP (which was not subject to a withdrawal penalty in this situation) to provide a monthly cash flow of $1,700; since they had planned and budgeted for it, they knew they had the money. When Robert turns fifty-nine and a half, he and Sharon will be able to draw additional funds from his IRAs without penalty. With more than $600,000 in total assets, they can make those withdrawals comfortably and without fear of the future.

Robert and Sharon now feel secure in and satisfied with their retirement. They are excited about the increase in income they will get from the IRAs and the extra income they will receive when they start drawing Social Security. Now that their finances are in order, they are set for life and can spend their time—and money—on what they choose. They plan to put the extra money toward world travel. They have a comfortable, albeit not extravagant, retirement for which they have planned well. They are in a position to choose whether or not they want to work. They are free to support their local church ministries and travel the world; next up for Robert and Sharon is a long stay in Europe.

On behalf of Retirement Benefits Institute, I implore you: Do all that you can to make your retirement story more like Robert and Sharon's than like Jim and Katherine's. Jim and Katherine were good people, and it is very unfortunate that they didn't get their finances in order sooner and that they didn't make the right decisions about their retirement.

So, the question is: What do you want for your retirement?

That's where you start. The rest of this book will serve as both map and guide to help you get where you want to be in retirement. The path is different for every retiree, but the journey always starts with educating yourself about your options.

CHAPTER 2

Navigating the Civil Service Retirement System

THE UNITED STATES government has several retirement systems that apply to federal employees. The Civil Service Retirement System (CSRS) is commonly referred to as the *old system*. Only employees hired before January 1, 1984, are eligible for CSRS. Federal employees hired after that date are covered under the Federal Employee Retirement System (FERS), the *new system*. CSRS was officially replaced by FERS in January 1987.

If you qualify for CSRS benefits, you have one of the best defined-benefit retirement package available in the United States! They simply don't make defined-benefit pensions like this anymore. If you haven't been grandfathered into the CSRS, you cannot get a CSRS annuity. If you are eligible, you have a serious retirement advantage in the form of a robust guaranteed annuity check for the rest of your life. However, the CSRS has some drawbacks. Unlike FERS employees, CSRS employees do not receive Social Security credits for their years of federal employment. CSRS employees can participate in the Thrift Savings Plan (TSP) to save additional tax-advantaged retirement funds, but the government does not match contributions for CSRS employees as it does for FERS employees. Despite these drawbacks, CSRS is still generally considered the better and more lucrative retirement package, and you still have many options for sheltering your personal retirement savings from taxes.

If you are a FERS employee, you can skip ahead to Chapter 3, where your retirement benefits are covered in more detail.

RETIREMENT ELIGIBILITY FOR A CSRS EMPLOYEE

Eligibility for CSRS is straightforward. If you were hired by the federal government before 1984, you are eligible for CSRS. However, CSRS has three different levels of retirement eligibility, based on an employee's age and length of service.

The earliest retirement age for a CSRS employee is fifty-five, but only with thirty years of service. A CSRS employee with twenty years of service may retire at age sixty with a full annuity, or at age sixty-two with a minimum of five years of service. (As of 2015, almost all CSRS employees have at least thirty years of service; the last CSRS was hired in 1983—thirty-two years ago.)

SPECIAL PROVISIONS ELIGIBILITY

Some employees with very demanding jobs—such as law enforcement officers, firefighters, and air traffic controllers—are covered under CSRS Special Provisions and are allowed to retire earlier than other CSRS employees without suffering penalties to their benefits. Special Provisions employees become eligible for retirement at age fifty with at least twenty years of Special Provision service. Air traffic controllers may also be eligible at any age with at least twenty-five years of federal service as an air traffic controller. Mandatory retirement ages apply for Special Provisions employees, meaning air traffic controllers are forced to retire at age fifty-six while firefighters and law enforcement officers must retire at age fifty-seven.

Virtually no federal employees are covered under the CSRS Special Provision rules anymore because most hired before 1984 have already retired.

A CSRS Retirement Age Eligibility	Special Provisions CSRS Retirement Age Eligibility
• Age 55 with 30 years of service	• Age 50 with 20 years of service
• Age 60 with 20 years of service	• Any age with 25 years of service (air traffic controllers only)
• Age 62 with 5 years of service	

CALCULATING YOUR CSRS ANNUITY

Two major components are required to calculate your CSRS annuity: your *high-three average* and your total years of service.

The high-three is the average of your highest-paid period of thirty-six consecutive months. This three-year period can be at any point in your career. Your regular pay, along with any locality pay, is included in the calculation for your high-three average.

However, certain additional pay during your high-three period is typically not included, such as bonuses, overtime, cash awards, military pay, and overseas cost-of-living adjustments. (We say "typically" because, in certain instances, some of these forms of additional pay may be included in your high-three, such as night differentials for wage-grade employees and law enforcement availability pay [LEAP], formerly known as Administratively Uncontrollable Overtime [AUO] for law enforcement.)

Depending on where you are in your career, you may not yet have hit your high-three and it may be necessary to estimate this number based on expected future earnings. If so, you should try to be conservative starting out—you can always adjust your estimated high-three upward later.

The second component of your CSRS annuity calculation is your total years of federal service. Most federal employees have some flexibility in choosing when to retire, and can calculate their total years of service based on their assumed retirement date.

Once you know your high-three and your total years of federal service, you can plug those numbers into the equations below to calculate your CSRS annuity. The high-three average incorporates a three-tiered calculation in its formula for determining your retirement annuity. You are paid the first-tier rate for the first years, the second-tier rate for the next years, and so on. (This is similar to the way income tax is calculated by brackets.)

The three tiers for calculating your CSRS annuity are:

- High-Three Average x 1.5 Percent x First Five Years of Service = Tier One Benefit
- High-Three Average x 1.75 Percent x Second Five Years of Service = Tier Two Benefit
- High-Three Average x 2 Percent x Additional Years of Service = Tier Three Benefit
- ○ **Total Annual Annuity Paid = Tier One + Tier Two + Tier Three**

Let's look at an example of one federal employee calculating his CSRS annuity. James retired from a federal agency at age sixty. His high-three average, which happened to fall at the end of his career, was $100,000. James worked at the same federal agency for thirty years before retiring in early February. Using the appropriate formula, James calculated his annuity benefit payment in this manner:

- $100,000 x 1.5 Percent x 5 = $7,500
- $100,000 x 1.75 Percent x 5 = $8,750
- $100,000 x 2 Percent x 20 = $40,000
- ○ **Total Sum of All Tiers = $56,250 Paid Annually, or $4,687.50 per Month**

The annuity formula for law enforcement officers, firefighters, and air traffic controllers who generally fall under Special Provisions is a little different. For example:

- High-Three x 2.5 Percent x First Twenty Years of Service = (A)
- High-Three x 2 Percent x Rest of Years of Service = (B)
- ○ A + B = Special Provisions Annual Annuity

SERVICE HISTORY ADJUSTMENTS

Several service-history issues may alter your annuity and retirement eligibility. Those service issues are: non-deduction service, refunded service, and military service.

Your service history may be adjusted by two primary mechanisms. You may have an adjustment to your retirement eligibility or how your service history is calculated into your annuity formula. The former is an adjustment to how many years you have accrued toward retirement eligibility, whereas the latter actually affects how your annuity will be calculated upon retirement. Let's look at the common types of service-history adjustments.

NON-DEDUCTION SERVICE

An employee may have non-deduction or non-deposit service from any point in their federal career. This refers to any period of service for which the employee was ineligible to make CSRS retirement contributions. Typically, the employee was working in either a temporary, seasonal, or Continuity of Operations status during the period of ineligibility. If you do not make retirement contributions, the time still counts as federal service. You can make the contributions for any non-deduction time afterward, and you may do so at any point in your career. You can request that your personnel office calculate the amount of the contribution for you.

The contribution will be the amount you would have paid into the CSRS retirement system and any interest accrued. If you make the contribution for your non-deduction time, the time will count toward your retirement eligibility and your annuity computation.

If you do not make the contribution, and your non-deduction time was before October 1, 1982, you will receive retirement eligibility credit, but your annuity will be reduced by 10 percent of the contribution you owe. For example, if you owe $3,000 for non-deduction service from before 1982 and do not pay your contribution, you will still receive credit for your service time, but your annuity will be reduced by $300 annually. If your non-deduction service was on or after October 1, 1982, and you do not pay the contribution, you will receive credit for retirement eligibility but not for your annuity computation.

This reduction in your annuity can be small or large, depending on the amount you owe. If you intend to pay your contribution, you should do so as soon as possible in order to avoid additional interest. A contribution of only a few hundred dollars could balloon to thousands of dollars if you wait twenty years to pay it. This could cause a noticeable reduction in your monthly annuity check!

—— PLANNING TIP ——

Buying this time back results in a great deal for employees, who will usually earn back their contribution in the form of a higher annuity in as little as two years.

REFUNDED SERVICE

When employees leave a federal government job before reaching retirement age, they have the option to take a refund for any CSRS contributions they have made. This is referred to as *refunded service.* If they later return to federal service, they may redeposit the contributions, plus interest; this action reinstates their retirement contributions and credits the previous federal service years as if they had never taken a refund.

Let's look at an example: Mary began her career as a CSRS employee. She worked for the federal government for ten years before deciding to leave for a job in the private sector. When she left federal service, she took the refund of her CSRS retirement contributions.

Several years later, Mary returned to work for the federal government. Upon her return, she was given the option to redeposit the contribution she took, plus interest. She chose to redeposit the funds and received annuity computation credit.

The point in service at which you take the refund will affect how your annuity is calculated if you don't redeposit the contributions. This is due to a change in the rules. If Mary had taken the refund before March 1, 1991, and chosen not to redeposit the contribution, she would have received retirement eligibility credit, but her annuity would have been actuarially reduced. If Mary had taken the refund on or after March 1, 1991, and chosen not to redeposit the contribution, she would have received retirement eligibility credit but not annuity computation credit. This means that her years of service would have counted toward her eligibility for retirement, but not her annuity computation, thereby reducing her annuity.

— PLANNING TIP —

It can take approximately ten years after retirement to earn back the redeposit for refunded service. For this reason, we advise making the redeposit only on a case-by-case basis. You definitely should have a professional calculate this to ensure that you choose what is best for you.

MILITARY SERVICE

CSRS employees have the opportunity to make a deposit for any active-duty military service. If you decide to pay the deposit—including interest—for your military time, you will receive both retirement eligibility and annuity computation credit for that time. Your military service will be treated exactly like any other CSRS-qualifying federal service, provided you make your contributions.

If you choose not to make the deposit, the date you were hired makes a difference in how your annuity is calculated after the age of sixty-two. If you were first hired under CSRS on or after October 1, 1982, and do not pay the deposit, you will not receive any credit for eligibility or annuity computation. If you were first hired under CSRS before October 1, 1982, you will receive credit for eligibility, but a special rule called Catch-62 applies to the annuity calculation.

Catch-62 states that those CSRS employees who did not make a deposit for any military service and will be eligible for Social Security when they reach age sixty-two will have their annuity calculated twice. The first calculation will be at your initial retirement and will include any military service time, even if you did not make a deposit. When you turn sixty-two, your annuity is recalculated and any military time is omitted from the calculation. If you are not eligible for Social Security at age sixty-two, then your annuity will not be calculated twice and you will be allowed to keep your annuity credits for military time served. As long as you were hired under CSRS before October 1, 1982, military service time counts toward retirement eligibility regardless of Social Security eligibility.

Note that the Catch-62 rule can work in your favor if you have not paid your deposit and will not be eligible for Social Security. If this is the case, you will get full credit for your military time without having to pay the deposit. If you know you will not be eligible for Social Security, you should not pay the military deposit, as you will still receive the annuity credit regardless.

It often benefits federal employees to pay their deposit and receive credit for military time. But if you are retired from the military or Catch-62 applies to you, it is usually not beneficial to make the deposit. You have to weigh your military pension against your CSRS annuity.

CSRS OFFSETS: BEST OF BOTH WORLDS

A CSRS offset annuity generally applies to any employee who served at least five years under CSRS, left service for one year or longer, and returned to service after January 1, 1984. CSRS offset annuities are calculated using the same formula for regular CSRS employees, but the annuity reduces at age sixty-two, when the employee becomes eligible for Social Security. This is because CSRS offset employees contribute to Social Security. This reduction always occurs at age sixty-two, regardless of whether the retiree begins drawing their Social Security benefit then or later. If retiring after age sixty-two, you will use the amount of Social Security that you are eligible for at that age in your offset formula.

To calculate your CSRS offset, take your Social Security benefit at age sixty-two and multiply it by the number of years you were a CSRS offset employee, and then divide by forty. This amount is your CSRS offset, which is subtracted from your CSRS annuity.

CSRS OFFSET FORMULA

Social Security Benefit at Age Sixty-Two x (Years as a CSRS Offset Employee ÷ Forty) = Offset Amount

---

If Lisa, a federal retiree, were subject to a CSRS offset, she could calculate it by using the above formula. If Lisa were entitled to a $1,500 Social Security benefit at age sixty-two and she spent ten years as a CSRS offset employee, she would be subject to a $375 monthly offset ($1,500 x 10 / 40) starting at the age of sixty-two, regardless of whether she drew on her Social Security. She would subtract this from her $3,046 per month CSRS annuity, bringing it down to $2,671 per month.

PART-TIME SERVICE

CSRS employees who have worked part time at any point in their careers will have their annuity prorated to reflect this fact. The reduction in your annuity is directly proportional to your reduced hours.

To calculate your prorated annuity, start by using the same annuity formula as all other CSRS employees, and then calculate your prorated factor. To do that, divide the total hours you actually worked as a CSRS employee throughout your entire career by the number of hours you would have worked if all of your service had been full time. (As per the Office of Personnel Management [OPM] rules, a year of full-time work equals 2,087 hours.) This is your prorated factor, which you can multiply by your annuity to find the prorated annuity that you will actually receive.

For example, suppose you worked as a CSRS employee for thirty years, but for some of those years you worked part time. Over the course of your career, you accrued only 58,000 hours.

Had you worked full time, you would have accrued 62,610 hours in that time (using OPM's rule that a full-time year equals 2,087 hours). To find your prorated factor, divide 58,000 by 62,610, giving you .93, or 93 percent. If your standard annuity was $3,000 per month, your prorated annuity in this scenario would be $2,790.

COST-OF-LIVING ADJUSTMENTS (COLAS)

CSRS retirees may receive cost-of-living adjustments (COLAs) on their annuity every January, beginning at retirement; the COLAs received by CSRS retirees are based on the Consumer Price Index for Urban Wage Earners and Clerical Workers (CPI-W). It is possible for the increase in the CPI-W to be 0, resulting in no COLA for that year. COLAs are a huge benefit and may keep inflation from eating away at your annuity over time.

There can be a considerable range in the CSRS COLA. At the writing of this book, the ten-year COLA average is 2.4 percent.

Very few retirees have pensions with such robust increases over their lifetimes. Those few retirees from the private sector who actually get a pension rarely enjoy COLAs. I have met many non-federal retirees and seen that their pension checks only cover the cost of health insurance!

MAXIMIZING YOUR ANNUITY

There are a few ways that you can maximize the money you will receive from your CSRS benefits. Chief among the strategies for doing so are choosing the best retirement date and using unused leave time wisely.

DON'T FORGET YOUR UNUSED LEAVE TIME!

One benefit that can increase your retirement annuity payment is any unused sick leave. If a CSRS employee has accumulated sick leave hours that were never utilized, these hours may be converted to service days, months, and years. Unused sick leave counts as time served, but it is not always a one-for-one conversion. You will need to reference the Credit for Unused Sick Leave Conversion Chart published by the Office of Personnel Management (OPM) in order to determine how many service days can be added to your calculation. The chart can be found on the opm.gov website. Make sure you understand the time that can be counted toward your creditable service calculation. Doing so can add real dollars to your monthly annuity.

Annual leave may not be used to boost your monthly annuity. However, if you have any unused annual leave at the time of your retirement, the federal government will buy it back and you will receive a lump-sum payment after retirement. To determine the amount of this lump sum, multiply your hours of unused annual leave by your current hourly rate.

This one-time payout is a boon that can help ease the transition into retirement, especially if it takes OPM six to nine months for final adjudication of your annuity. Some retirees like to leave at the end of the year so that this lump sum is received in the following tax year, and hopefully taxed at a lower rate. Unfortunately, many CSRS retirees will not actually fall into a lower marginal tax bracket (see Chapter 8 on taxes for more information).

PICKING YOUR RETIREMENT DATE

The best days for CSRS employees to retire are typically either the first three days of the month or the last day of the month. Retiring on one of these four days results in your annuity becoming effective *the very next day*. Once your annuity becomes effective, you will be paid one month later for the previous month's benefit.

If you retire on any other day of the month, your annuity will not become effective until the first day of the subsequent month and you will not receive your annuity check until the following month. This will result in up to a two-month wait to get your first check, and you will effectively forfeit any benefits for the month during which you are not working but also not accruing benefits.

For an example of how this works, let's look again at Lisa. If Lisa retires on January 31, February 1, February 2, or February 3, her annuity will become effective the following day and she will receive his first payment at the beginning of March. However, if Lisa waits until February 4 to retire, her annuity will not become effective until March 1, and she will not receive her first payment until April. Effectively, her benefit from the month of February is lost and can never be recovered.

YOU HAVE THE BEST DEFINED-BENEFIT PENSION IN THE WORLD—NOW WHAT?

Now that you have read this chapter, you should be able to determine whether or not you are eligible for CSRS benefits and how to calculate your annuity payments based on your years of service, your high-three, and the many other variables. You also know the techniques you can use to maximize your benefit by retiring at the right time in the right way. In essence, you should understand exactly how the CSRS works and to whom it pertains.

However, this is only the tip of the iceberg of what you need to know in order to plan and realize a successful retirement. There is more to retirement than calculating your annuity. You also need to understand how your CSRS annuity fits into your entire retirement financial picture. This means understanding what your retirement income will be and drawing up a basic budget. Even if your retirement income meets or exceeds your working pay, you still need a budget in order to make sure that you are making the most of your retirement income and maximizing your lifestyle. (Not a bad problem to have!)

You also need to develop a firm understanding of the tax implications of your CSRS annuity. A large annuity can equate to a large tax burden. Again, this is a good problem to have, but that doesn't mean you can ignore the tax implications of your retirement income.

These are the topics of subsequent chapters in this book. We implore you to read on to understand how your CSRS benefits fit into your overall retirement picture. The following chapter is about the Federal Employees Retirement System (FERS), which is one of the newer benefit systems for federal employees hired in recent decades. If you are 100 percent certain that you are eligible only for CSRS and are not covered by FERS, you can skip the next chapter since it does not pertain to you. However, much of the rest of this book will still be relevant to you because it covers many other components of your federal retirement package, as well as how to navigate the tax system, budgeting, TSP, Medicare, and more.

CHAPTER 3

Navigating the Federal Employees
Retirement System

IN 1987, THE federal government introduced a new retirement system for federal employees—the Federal Employees Retirement System (FERS). Most federal employees hired on or after January 1, 1984, are covered under FERS. Many people consider FERS less lucrative than CSRS, but in truth FERS benefits can be just as advantageous if you understand all of the options available to you and work to maximize your benefits. Helping you do just that is the focus of this chapter.

FERS employees receive a smaller annuity than CSRS employees. To compensate for the decreased pension, FERS employees contribute to Social Security and can generally start taking benefits as early as age sixty-two. Although employees under both systems may take part in the Thrift Savings Plan (TSP, the federal government's 401[k] program), only FERS employees are incentivized to do so. FERS employees who contribute at least 5 percent per pay period receive an employer match of 5 percent of the employee's pay.

ARE YOU ELIGIBLE TO RETIRE?

Retirement eligibility for a FERS employee is determined by age and length of service. With at least thirty years of service, FERS employees may retire at their minimum retirement age (MRA) with full benefits. However, some employees may not plan to work a full thirty years. For this reason, there are two other eligibility options: FERS employees with at least twenty years of service may retire at age sixty, and any FERS employee may retire at age sixty-two with at least five years of service, in both cases with full benefits. Even with thirty years of service, you must still wait until your MRA to retire if you immediately want full benefits. An employee's minimum retirement age is dependent on the year they were born. See the chart on the following page to calculate your MRA:

| MINIMUM RETIREMENT AGE (MRA) CALCULATION CHART ||
Birth Year	MRA
1947 and earlier	55 years
1948	55 years and 2 months
1949	55 years and 4 months
1950	55 years and 6 months
1951	55 years and 8 months
1952	55 years and 10 months
1953–1964	56 years
1965	56 years and 2 months
1966	56 years and 4 months
1967	56 years and 6 months
1968	56 years and 8 months
1969	56 years and 10 months
1970 and later	57 years

SPECIAL PROVISIONS ELIGIBILITY

Some employees with very demanding jobs, such as law enforcement officers, firefighters, and air traffic controllers, are covered under FERS Special Provisions and are allowed to retire earlier than other FERS employees without suffering penalties to their benefits. Special Provisions employees become eligible for retirement at age fifty with at least twenty years of Special Provision service, or at any age with at least twenty-five years of service, at least twenty of which must be Special Provisions service.

Mandatory retirement ages apply for Special Provisions employees, meaning air traffic controllers are forced to retire at age fifty-six, while firefighters and law enforcement officers must retire at age fifty-seven.

NEED TO LEAVE EARLY? MRA+10 PROVISION

Federal employees who wish to retire early may do so under the MRA+10 Provision. Under this provision, an employee having reached MRA may retire with only ten years of service, rather than the typical thirty service years, in exchange for a reduction in their FERS pension. If you retire under this provision, you will be subject to a 5 percent penalty for every year that you retire under age sixty-two. For example, if you retired under this provision at age fifty-six, your annuity would be reduced by 5 percent for each of the six years you retired early, resulting in a 30 percent reduction in your annuity.

The MRA+10 Provision allows you to avoid lost benefits associated with early federal retirement. You will not get to keep continuous life insurance (Federal Employees Group Life Insurance [FEGLI]) and health coverage (Federal Employees Health Benefits [FEHB]) unless you postpone the receipt of your annuity until you reach age sixty (for employees with twenty years of service) or age sixty-two (for employees with ten to nineteen years of service). During the postponement period you will lose FEHB and FEGLI, but will be able to pick them back up once you have met both age and service requirements. Another caveat about taking the MRA+10 is that retiring under this provision makes you ineligible to receive the FERS Special Retirement Supplement—a monthly supplemental benefit used to bridge the gap between retirement and age sixty-two. We will discuss the Special Retirement Supplement in more detail later in the chapter.

CALCULATING YOUR FERS ANNUITY

What most FERS employees want to know is: *What will my annuity be when I retire?* Calculating your FERS annuity starts with determining two main variables—your high-three average and your total years of service.

The high-three is the average of your highest-paid period of thirty-six consecutive months. This three-year period can be at any point in your career. Your regular pay, along with any locality pay, is included in the calculation for your high-three average.

However, certain additional pay during your high-three period is typically not included, such as bonuses, overtime, cash awards, military pay, and overseas cost-of-living adjustments. (We say "typically" because, in certain instances, some of these forms of additional pay may be included in your high-three, such as night differentials for wage-grade employees and law enforcement availability pay [LEAP], formerly known as Administratively Uncontrollable Overtime [AUO] for law enforcement.)

Depending on where you are in your career, you may not yet have hit your high-three and it may be necessary to estimate this number based on expected future earnings. If so, you should try to be conservative starting out—you can always adjust your estimated high-three upward later.

The second component of your FERS annuity calculation is your total years of federal service. Employees planning for retirement can calculate this number based on their assumed retirement date. For some employees, such as air traffic controllers, who are subject to mandatory retirement dates, this may be fairly obvious. But most federal employees have some flexibility in choosing when to retire.

Once you know your high-three and total years of federal service, you can calculate your annuity by plugging those numbers into one of the following equations. Three separate formulas exist for calculating most FERS annuities: the standard FERS annuity formula; the enhanced FERS annuity formula for FERS employees who retire at age sixty-two or older with at least twenty years of service; and the FERS Special Provisions formula for law enforcement officers, firefighters, and air traffic controllers.

➤ **Standard FERS Annuity Formula:**
- High-Three x 1 Percent x Years of Service = Annual Annuity

➤ **Enhanced FERS Annuity Formula:**
- High-Three x 1.1 Percent x Years of Service = Annual Annuity

➤ **Special Provisions FERS Annuity Formula:**
- High-Three x 1.7 Percent x First Twenty Years of Service = (A)
- High-Three x 1 Percent x Rest of Years of Service = (B)

○ **A + B = Special Provisions Annual Annuity**

For an example of how to calculate your FERS annuity, let's consider the case of Darren, a FERS employee who retired at age sixty from his administrative job with a federal agency after thirty years of service. His high-three average is $100,000. Under the FERS system, Darren's first gross monthly annuity check will come to $2,500 ($100,000 x 1% x 30 = $30,000 annually, or $2,500 per month). If Darren waits until age sixty-two to retire, he will rack up two more years of service *and* be allowed to retire under the enhanced FERS annuity formula. Let's assume that his high-three average has now increased to $103,000; this raises his gross monthly annuity to $3,021 ($103,000 x 1.1% x 32 = $36,256 annually, or $3,021 per month).

SERVICE HISTORY

Several service history issues may alter your annuity calculation and eligibility. They are: non-deduction service, refunded service, and military service.

There are two primary mechanisms by which your service history may be adjusted. You may have an adjustment to your *retirement eligibility* and/or how your *service history* is calculated. The former is an adjustment to how many years you have accrued toward retirement eligibility, whereas the latter actually affects how your annuity will be calculated at retirement. These adjustments may be made in conjunction or independently of one another, depending on your situation.

Let's now take a look at the common types of service history adjustments.

NON-DEDUCTION SERVICE

FERS employees may have non-deduction or non-deposit service from any point in their careers. This refers to any period of service for which the employee was ineligible to make FERS retirement contributions. Typically, the employee was working in either a temporary, seasonal, or Continuity of Operations status during the period of ineligibility. This time does not count toward your federal service for retirement purposes.

However, if you have accrued non-deduction time prior to January 1, 1989, you may have the opportunity to make the deposit for that time. If you make the deposit for your non-deduction time, the time will count toward your retirement eligibility and your annuity computation. The contribution will be the amount you would have paid into the FERS retirement system plus any interest accrued. You can request that your personnel office calculate the amount of the contribution for you.

Failure to make the contribution will result in a smaller annuity and a longer period for eligibility. This reduction in your annuity can be small or large, depending on the amount you owe. If you intend to pay your contribution, you should do so as soon as possible to avoid additional interest. A contribution of only a few hundred dollars paid immediately could balloon to thousands of dollars if you wait twenty or thirty years to pay it. This could cause a noticeable reduction in your monthly annuity check!

— PLANNING TIP —

In our experience, buying this time back results in a great deal for the employee, who will usually come out ahead in as little as two years after retirement. After this time, the increase in your annuity will make up for what you spent on the buyback.

REFUNDED SERVICE

When employees leave the federal government before retirement age, they have the option to take a refund for any FERS contributions they have made. This is referred to as *refunded service*. If they later return to federal service, they may redeposit the contributions, plus interest; this action reinstates their retirement contributions and credits the federal service years as if they had never taken a refund.

Let's look at an example of an employee who received a refund and then redeposited the refunded contributions. Tom began his career in the federal government as a FERS employee. He worked for ten years before deciding to leave the federal government for a job in the private sector. At that time, he was given the option to receive a refund of his FERS retirement contributions, which he decided to take. Several years later, Tom returned to work for the federal government. Upon his return, he was permitted to redeposit the refund of contributions he had taken, with interest. He decided to make the full redeposit so that he could receive both retirement eligibility and annuity computation credit. If he had decided not to make the redeposit, he would still receive credit for retirement eligibility for the years worked, but not for annuity computation purposes.

MILITARY SERVICE (ON OR AFTER JANUARY 1, 1957)

FERS employees have the opportunity to make a deposit for active-duty military service so that their military time will be treated as federal service for purposes of FERS benefits. If you decide to pay the deposit, including interest, for your military time, you will receive retirement eligibility and annuity computation credit. In other words, your time served in the military can function exactly the same as time served as a FERS employee. If you do not make a deposit for your military time, you will not receive retirement eligibility or annuity computation credit.

Many (but not all) employees will benefit from making the deposit and receiving FERS service history credit for their military time. If you are retired from the military, it is usually not beneficial to make the deposit, because it likely means giving up your military pension and other benefits upon your FERS retirement.

It is always up to you to make sure your service history is accurate. Consider the case of Andy, a FERS employee with some military time. He was ready to retire with what he thought was thirty years of service. The service computation date (SCD) on his pay stub said he had thirty years, but Andy didn't realize that this included some military service he had not made a deposit for.

At this point, Andy had two options: make a deposit for the military time or continue to work another six months. Because interest accrued had caused the deposit to balloon, he reluctantly opted to postpone retirement and serve another six months in order to obtain his thirty years.

Let this be a cautionary tale: *You* are responsible for the accuracy of your service history. Your pay stub has an SCD on it that is for *leave* purposes. This date may or may not be the right date for *retirement* purposes. Make sure you know the difference.

FERS TRANSFERS

FERS transfers are federal employees who had at least 5 years of creditable civilian service but switched over to FERS after it was created. They are subject to the same rules and regulations as regular FERS employees, with one exception: Their annuity *is* calculated differently, depending on how many years of CSRS service they performed.

FERS transfers will have two components to their annuity—one for the CSRS years served and another for the FERS portion of their service. These annuities are calculated separately. To calculate the CSRS portion, please see the CSRS formulas in Chapter 2 of this book. The FERS portion is calculated based on the formulas in this chapter. When calculating your annuity, you may not count years twice or shift FERS-covered years over into CSRS, or vice versa. FERS transfers who have accumulated less than five years of service under the CSRS system will have their annuity calculated as if all of their service was under FERS. For all intents and purposes, FERS transfers with less than five years of service are treated exactly like any other FERS employee.

For purposes of retirement eligibility, FERS transfers may count all of their federal service history, regardless of which system it was accrued under.

PART-TIME SERVICE

FERS employees who have worked part time at any point in their careers will have their annuity prorated to reflect this fact. The reduction in your annuity is directly proportional to your reduced hours.

To calculate your prorated annuity, start by using the same annuity formula as all other FERS employees, and then calculate your prorated factor. To do that, divide the total hours you actually worked as a FERS employee over your entire career by the number of hours you would have worked if all of your service were full time. (As per the OPM rules, a year of full-time work equals 2,087 hours.) This is your prorated factor, which you can multiply by your annuity to find the prorated annuity that you will actually receive.

For example, suppose you worked as a FERS employee for thirty years, but for some of those years you worked part time. Over the course of your career, you accrued only 58,000 hours. Had you worked full time, you would have accrued 62,610 hours in that time (using the OPM assumption that a full-time year equals 2,087 hours). To find your prorated factor, you would divide 58,000 by 62,610, giving you .93, or 93 percent. If your standard annuity was $3,000 per month, your monthly prorated annuity in this scenario would be $2,790.

COST-OF-LIVING ADJUSTMENTS (COLAS)

FERS retirees are among the last few Americans who still get regular pay raises during retirement. FERS retirees may receive a cost-of-living adjustment (COLA) on their annuity each year to help keep pace with inflation. Generally, COLAs for regular FERS retirees start at age sixty-two. FERS Special Provisions retirees start receiving COLAs as soon as they retire, with the exception of air traffic controllers retiring under the "Vision 100" option.

At the writing of this book, COLAs are based on the increases in the Consumer Price Index for Urban Wage Earners and Clerical

Workers (CPI-W), though the COLA is not equal to the CPI-W. It is possible for CPI-W to be 0 , resulting in no COLA for that year. The chart below illustrates how the FERS COLA is determined depending on the CPI-W:

DETERMINING THE FERS COLA	
When the CPI-W increase is:	The FERS COLA is:
> 3%	CPI-W increase – 1%
2–3%	2%
≤ 2%	CPI-W increase

There can be a considerable range in the FERS COLA. Over the last ten years, the FERS COLA has ranged between 0 and 4.8 percent, averaging out to 1.97 percent over that period.

Very few retirees have pensions with such robust increases over their lifetimes. Those rare retirees from the private sector who actually get a pension rarely enjoy COLAs. I have met many non-federal retirees and seen that their pension checks only cover the cost of health insurance!

MAXIMIZING YOUR ANNUITY

There are a few ways that you can maximize the money you will receive from your FERS benefits. Chief among the strategies for doing so are choosing the best retirement date and using unused leave time wisely.

DON'T LEAVE YOUR LEAVE TIME ON THE TABLE!

Recently the government noticed a funny discrepancy between how CSRS and FERS employees were using their sick leave as they neared retirement. While CSRS employees were working diligently all the way until the end of their careers, FERS employees tended to suddenly and mysteriously come down with various afflictions in their last year of employment. The reason? CSRS employees were allowed to add their sick leave to their annuity calculation and receive credit for these hours. FERS employees were not allowed to do this, and with no incentive not to use their sick leave, as they neared retirement they found creative ways to use the hours.

Thankfully, the rules have changed and FERS employees retiring after January 1, 2014, may add all of their unused sick leave to their annuity computation, just like CSRS employees.

Unused sick leave counts as time served, but it is not a one-for-one conversion. You will need to reference the Credit for Unused Sick Leave Conversion Chart published by the Office of Personnel Management (OPM) to determine how many service days can be added to your calculation. The chart can be found online at opm.gov.

In addition to sick leave, you may also have unused annual leave at retirement. Annual leave may not be used to boost your monthly annuity. However, if you have any unused annual leave at retirement, the federal government will buy it back and you will receive a lump-sum payment after retirement.

To determine the amount of this lump sum, multiply your hours of unused annual leave by your current hourly rate. This one-time payout is a boon that can help ease the transition into retirement, especially if it takes OPM six to nine months for final adjudication of your annuity. Some retirees like to leave at the end of the year so that this lump sum is received after retirement, and hopefully taxed at a lower rate. Unfortunately, many FERS retirees will not actually fall into a lower tax bracket. (See Chapter 8 on taxes for more information.)

CHOOSING YOUR RETIREMENT DATE

The best day for FERS employees to retire is typically the last day of the month. Your FERS annuity begins to accrue on the first day of the following month after you retire. If you retire on the last day of the month, your annuity benefits will begin to accrue the very next day.

If you miss the last day of the month and wait until the first day of the next month to retire, your annuity will not become effective until the first day of the subsequent month and you will not receive your annuity check until the following month. This will result in a two-month wait to get your first check, and you will effectively be forfeiting any benefits for the month in which you are not working.

To illustrate how this works, we provide the following example: If Lucy retires from her job with the federal government on January 31, her annuity will become effective February 1 and her benefits will accrue for all of February. She will receive her first annuity check in early March.

However, if Lucy waits until February 1 to retire, her annuity will not become effective until March 1, and she will not receive her first annuity check until early April. Her February benefits are gone and lost forever. That is a steep price to pay just for clocking in at work an extra day!

EXTRA! EXTRA! SPECIAL RETIREMENT SUPPLEMENT

FERS employees contribute to and receive payments from the Social Security system as a way to offset the reduced annuity under the new system. Unlike CSRS employees, who get a larger annuity, FERS employees often need Social Security payments to supplement their retirement income. However, FERS employees generally cannot start drawing Social Security until they are sixty-two, even if they retire earlier.

To bridge the gap between the time of retirement and Social Security eligibility, the government offers FERS employees a Special Retirement Supplement (SRS), which provides supplemental monthly income. Your FERS SRS benefit does not affect your Social Security benefit in any way whatsoever. The SRS ends at age sixty-two, even if you decide to delay the receipt of your Social Security benefit.

For those who retire early, the SRS benefit is an important supplement. However, as we mentioned earlier in this chapter, employees who retire under the MRA+10 Provision are ineligible for SRS. You have to retire with a normal full annuity to be eligible for this benefit. Because your SRS benefit will expire at age sixty-two, you should talk to a financial professional about the optimal time to start drawing Social Security. If you delay drawing Social Security past the age of sixty-two, you will later receive larger Social Security checks, but you may have to draw on assets to cover your income needs during that period. Deciding when to start drawing Social Security is a major and personal decision that depends on several factors of your individual finances. (For more information on Social Security, please see Chapter 5.)

The federal government calculates your SRS benefit based on a standardized formula. You will need to know what your Social Security benefit will be when you turn sixty-two, and you will need to know how many years of service you are credited with under the FERS retirement system. Please note that, unlike the FERS annuity, the SRS benefit does *not* include military time as qualifying service, regardless of whether you paid the deposit to include your military time in your FERS annuity. The SRS benefit also does not receive any cost-of-living adjustment, though this is not usually a major burden since it expires when you turn sixty-two.

FERS SPECIAL RETIREMENT SUPPLEMENT FORMULA

Social Security Benefit at Age Sixty-Two x (Number of FERS Service Years ÷ Forty) = Monthly Benefit

---

Consider the following example of one FERS employee calculating her SRS benefit. Janet wanted to retire from her government position at age fifty-six, following twenty-five years of

FERS service. She also served five years in the military prior to her FERS employment, and while she paid the deposit for these five years and will receive annuity credit and retirement eligibility, it will not count for her FERS SRS benefit. When Janet turns sixty-two, she will be eligible for $1,200 per month in Social Security benefits. Based on this information, Janet would be eligible for a FERS SRS benefit of $750 per month, or $9,000 annually ($1,200 x [25 ÷ 40] = $750 per month).

While the FERS SRS benefit does not affect your Social Security, the benefit does follow the same earnings-test rules that apply to Social Security. This means that earning income in retirement beyond a certain threshold can decrease your SRS benefit. Special Provisions employees are exempt from the earnings test until they have reached their minimum retirement age. (Note: Your *minimum* retirement age may be different from your *mandatory* retirement age.)

The earnings test states that for every two dollars you earn over the limit, one dollar will be withheld from your SRS benefit. The earnings limit for 2015 is $15,720. The limit is typically adjusted for inflation annually. Visit the Retirement Benefits Institute website for the latest figures.

http://retireinstitute.com
/resources/helpful-links/

Not all earnings count against your SRS benefit—only those earnings generated from a wage, like what you might earn from that Walmart greeter job you've always dreamed of. Generally, the only income that counts is that for which you would receive a W-2, certain 1099s, or similar IRS forms for reporting earned income. Your FERS annuity, withdrawals from tax-deferred savings (TSP, IRA, etc), and even investment income do not apply toward the SRS benefit-earnings limit.

For an example of how your SRS can be reduced or even eliminated, consider the case of Janet. She is entitled to a FERS SRS benefit of $9,000. The following chart illustrates how various levels of income will affect her SRS benefit based upon 2015 numbers:

JANET'S POST-RETIREMENT JOB ANNUAL INCOME	JANET'S ANNUAL SRS
$10,000	$9,000
$20,000	$6,860
$34,000	$0

As you can see, Janet will receive a full SRS benefit if she earns only $10,000 in wages because that places her below the $15,720 threshold. However, if Janet earns $20,000 as a part-time freelancer in retirement, she will be $4,280 over the limit. Half of this overage amount will be deducted from her SRS, leaving her with an SRS benefit of only $6,860. If Janet earns $34,000, her SRS benefit will be reduced to zero.

Whether or not to work in retirement is a personal decision. Many people want or need to work in retirement for all kinds of financial and personal reasons. If you know you will need more income than the stated earnings limit allows, by all means, earn as much as you need. Clearly, Janet's $34,000 income is much higher than the $9,000 she would receive annually in SRS.

— PLANNING TIP —

Understand how your post-retirement employment may affect your SRS. Be careful not to count on both if you go over the limit.

BEYOND FERS: THE THREE-LEGGED STOOL

After reading this chapter, you should understand whether or not you are eligible for FERS benefits and how to calculate your annuity payments based on your years of service, your high-three, and any service history adjustments. You also know the techniques that will enable you to maximize your benefit by retiring at the right time. In essence, you should understand exactly how FERS works.

However, this is only the tip of the iceberg of what you will need to know in order to plan for a successful retirement. Your FERS benefits are only one component of your retirement package, and planning for the future requires you to do more than simply calculate your annuity. FERS employees construct a retirement income from their annuity, Social Security, and their personal savings (which includes the TSP). Financial professionals often refer to this triumvirate as the "three-legged stool."

All three legs are important to maximizing your retirement income, but they will not necessarily bear the same weight in your planning, nor do they have to. That's the beauty of having multiple income streams—one leg can compensate for the others. For example, if you haven't put enough away in savings, you can continue working longer to beef up your pension and delay drawing Social Security in order to increase your benefit.

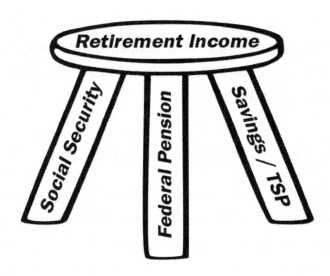

There are various strategies you can employ when planning for retirement, but you must understand your entire financial situation and your options. You also need to develop a firm understanding of what the tax implications of your FERS annuity and other income will be, and how the different components of your retirement will work together. The three legs of the stool can and do affect one another. Plan so that these legs work with rather than against one another.

These topics and more are covered in detail in the following chapters. We implore you to read on to understand how your FERS benefits fit into your overall federal retirement package and personal retirement finances.

CHAPTER 4

Survivor Benefits: Taking Care of the Ones You Love

WHILE NO ONE likes to contemplate their own death, making sure that your family will be provided for after your passing is an important part of retirement planning. Private-sector employees generally just apply for and buy life insurance and move on, but as a federal employee you have special options that must be carefully weighed. Some of the biggest choices about insurance and survivor benefits are still ahead of you.

The federal government provides two kinds of survivor benefits: the basic employee death benefit, and the monthly annuity. These provide some measure of death benefit to a surviving beneficiary. Neither has anything to do with your Federal Employees Group Life Insurance (FEGLI) benefits, which are discussed in Chapter 9 of this book. Let's look at them both separately.

PASSING AWAY WHILE STILL EMPLOYED

Most federal employees are not aware of their basic survivor benefit because you need only be eligible for the benefit to receive it—no enrollment is required. This is a life insurance benefit for federal employees who die while still in service.

For your spouse to be eligible for basic survivor benefits, you must have been married for at least nine months. Those requirements are waived if there was a child born of the marriage or if the employee's death was accidental. Former spouses may qualify for this benefit if they have a qualifying court order on file with OPM and they were married to the deceased employee for at least nine months and have not remarried before the age of fifty-five.

THE BENEFIT FOR FERS EMPLOYEES

For FERS employees who die while still employed on or after December 1, 2011, the survivor benefit is equal to the higher of: 50 percent of their final salary or their high-three average, plus a lump-sum payment of $30,792. (The amount of the lump payment, put into place in 2011, is subject to change.) This is a one-time payout. In order to be eligible for this benefit, you must have completed eighteen months of creditable civilian service.

If the employee has completed ten years of creditable service by the time of death, the beneficiary will also receive a monthly benefit in addition to the basic benefit. This monthly benefit is 50 percent of the employee's basic annuity at their death.

THE BENEFIT FOR CSRS EMPLOYEES

In the case of CSRS employees, beneficiaries do not get a lump-sum basic benefit (such as FERS employees' beneficiaries receive), but they are eligible for a monthly benefit if the deceased employee has completed eighteen months of creditable service.

This monthly basic benefit for CSRS employees is 55 percent of the higher of: their annuity computed under the general formula, *or* a "guaranteed minimum," which is the lesser of 40 percent of the employee's high-three salary or the regular annuity obtained after increasing the deceased employee's length of service by the period of time between the date of death and the date he or she would have been age sixty.

MINOR CHILDREN AND THE BASIC BENEFIT

Minor children are eligible for a monthly annuity under the basic benefit until they turn age eighteen, marry, or die. Their benefits can continue until age twenty-two if they are full-time students. Unmarried, disabled, dependent children may receive the recurring monthly benefits, if the disability occurred before age eighteen.

The exact amount of this monthly annuity for minor children depends upon whether the child has a living parent who was married to the employee. This amount is reduced dollar for dollar by any Social Security children's benefits that may be payable.

PASSING AWAY IN RETIREMENT: THE SURVIVOR ANNUITY

Now let's assume you *don't* die while working and you do get to retire! Your beneficiary will still get a death benefit, but it is different from the one you "missed out on" by living into retirement!

All federal retirees are eligible for a survivor annuity option. This benefit option provides a portion of your annuity to the named survivor upon your death, typically your spouse. Unlike the survivor benefits while working, the survivor annuity is not automatic or required. You must make your survivor annuity election at the time you submit your retirement paperwork. You may choose a full, partial, or no benefit based upon your needs. FERS employees may choose to leave their surviving spouse 0 percent, 25 percent, or 50 percent. CSRS employees have more options: they can elect to provide up to 55 percent of their annuity benefit to their survivor.

There is a cost to taking the survivor annuity, which results in a lower benefit amount paid to you. FERS employees who take a 50 percent survivor benefit will have their own annuity reduced by 10 percent, and those who opt for a 25 percent survivor annuity will have their annuity reduced by 5 percent. CSRS employees can elect to leave any amount of benefit to their survivor, up to 55 percent of their annuity, at a small cost of 2.5 percent on the first $3,600 plus the heftier 10 percent cost for any amount over that.

The majority of federal employees we meet do not realize they have different options when it comes to their death benefits. Consequently, they have not given the options much thought. We encourage you to be a wise consumer here, and consider your options before electing this benefit so that you are confident you are doing what is best for you and your family.

THE SURVIVOR ANNUITY VS. LIFE INSURANCE

The survivor annuity is not life insurance, but it can function in much the same way when it comes to financial planning.

Think about it this way: you take the survivor annuity option, and when you die, you leave your spouse a benefit. That sounds an awful lot like life insurance, doesn't it? It sure does! Both can fulfill similar functions, which is why they should be considered in conjunction with each other.

Whether a survivor annuity option or a private life insurance policy is right for you depends on your individual situation. The chart below provides a mere glimpse of some of the primary differences between life insurance and the survivor annuity. For more detailed information, view our video at the RBI website.

http://retireinstitute.com
/survivor-benefits/

SURVIVOR BENEFITS OPTIONS		
	Life Insurance	Survivor Annuity
Payment Options	Lump sum or annuity	Annuity only
Flexibility/Control	Yes	No
Cost	Based on age and health	Standardized
Taxes	Tax-free death benefit	Partially taxable benefit
Health Insurance Continuation	No, must choose minimum survivor annuity	Yes
Changing Beneficiaries	Yes	Typically, no
Inflation Protection	Maybe, depending on the type of insurance purchased	Yes, to some extent

The key thing to understand about the above chart is there is no right or wrong decision—at least not one that applies to everyone. It is simply a set of choices, each with its own pros and cons. For some people, life insurance is better. For others, taking a full survivor annuity is the way to go. For others still, some combination of the survivor annuity and a life insurance policy might make the most financial sense. Understand the repercussions of your choices before you make them in order to maximize your benefits.

Do not forget that there are costs associated with the survivor annuity, just as with life insurance. Taking this benefit reduces your own annuity forever (unless, of course, your spouse dies first). You should carefully weigh the reduction in your annuity against the cost of purchasing a private life insurance policy before making a final selection. This can be a complex set of trade-offs, and we recommend seeing an insurance professional for a needs analysis.

COLAS: THE DOUBLE-EDGED SWORD

Survivor annuity monthly benefits may receive cost-of-living adjustments (COLAs) every year, which helps keep up with inflation. For the last ten years, ending in 2015, the average ten-year CSRS COLA has been 2.4 percent per year. The FERS ten-year COLA was 1.97 percent (we call this "diet COLA"). A survivor benefit with a COLA is a unique perk.

However, the COLA is a double-edged sword. You also receive COLAs on your pension while you are living. Because taking the survivor annuity reduces your pension, electing to take this benefit reduces the overall COLA received on your annuity. Taking this benefit means you lose that COLA, and the compounding effect of the next year's COLA, and the next year's ... and so on. This lost benefit grows ever larger over time. In addition, as COLAs apply, the annuity increases, thus the survivor annuity and cost also increase with it.

Is it possible to forgo the survivor annuity and use the money saved to buy a private life insurance policy that provides a death benefit without a rising cost structure baked into it? It depends on your situation and insurability. But we recommend that you analyze the costs and benefits of all options carefully.

STOP! WILL YOUR SURVIVING SPOUSE NEED YOUR HEALTH BENEFITS?

Your health insurance needs are a major consideration when choosing what kind of death benefits you need in retirement. For your spouse to continue on your Federal Employees Health Benefits (FEHB) plan after you die, you'll need to leave them some minimum level of survivor benefits. For this reason, most federal employees carry at least the minimum amount of survivor annuity benefit, even if they don't need the income replacement at death. If this health coverage is important to you, consider taking at least the minimum survivor benefit.

STOP AGAIN! ARE YOU EVEN INSURABLE?

You cannot just assume that you will be able to buy any private policy you want—you must qualify. Life insurance is first purchased with your health, then your money. Poor health can result in higher life insurance premiums and even denial of coverage, which in some cases can make the survivor annuity the more cost-effective option. Good health can have the opposite effect. The survivor annuity is not subject to these conditions—you're automatically eligible for coverage at a standard 10 percent cost.

BE A WISE CONSUMER

There is no easy way to determine which of the various levels of survivor annuity benefit and life insurance options is best for you;

it ultimately comes down to a matter of personal choice. There is no right or wrong answer, and without performing a needs analysis, I cannot tell individual readers of this book what options are best for them. Instead, we offer an example of how the different considerations play out for one hypothetical federal employee.

Let's consider the case of Frank, who, like many federal employees, wants to make sure his family is taken care of in the event of his death. As a CSRS employee, he will get a substantial annuity when he retires at age fifty-eight. He is struggling with his survivor annuity options for his wife, Pam, who is also age fifty-eight. He knows he can get a higher annuity benefit for the rest of his life if he does not choose a survivor annuity, but he also does not want Pam to struggle if he predeceases her.

As a CSRS employee, Frank can choose any percent of the survivor benefit amount as we discussed earlier—from 0 percent to 55 percent. (Note: FERS employees can choose 50 percent, 25 percent, or 0 percent.) The chart below displays some of Frank's choices regarding his annuity options:

SURVIVOR MONTHLY BENEFIT

High-Three = $93,832	Years of Service = 32.5
Frank's monthly annuity without survivor annuity	$4,789
Frank's monthly annuity with survivor annuity	$4,333
Pam's monthly survivor annuity (55 percent)	$2,634
Frank's monthly cost of survivor annuity	$456

PENSION MAXIMIZATION

It may be possible for Frank to take the higher annuity and still be able to provide for his wife's security in the event of his passing. He can use what is commonly called *pension maximization,* which uses life insurance to replace a portion of Frank's annuity at his death. This requires, in part, estimating how much Frank is *likely* to pay if he opts for a private policy instead of the survivor benefit option.

Pension maximization starts by estimating the future value of your spouse's survivor annuity. In Frank's case, we multiply $2,634 by a predetermined multiple based on Pam's age. In this way, we are able to estimate the future value of Pam's survivor benefit, which comes out to approximately $525,000. (We are omitting the calculation because it is complex, varies per individual, and provides only an estimate—you need to see a professional for this.)

Once Frank knows the value of the annuity, he may be able to use a combination of term and permanent life insurance policies to replace this future value. By looking at the premiums, he can compare the costs of private policies with the costs of the survivor annuity.

The following chart provides sample hypothetical rates for different types of life insurance. Please note that these rates are intended simply to illustrate the concept and should not be used to estimate personal costs and benefits. Your own rates may vary; again, you need to see an insurance professional. The quotes shown in the chart below assume a standard health rating for a fifty-eight-year-old male:

POLICY RATES

Type of LI	Policy Length	Amount of Coverage	Monthly Premium
Universal Life	Permanent	$200,000	$333
Term	10-Year	$300,000	$130

Disclaimer: The table above is hypothetical and for illustrative purposes only.

A ten-year term policy may be sufficient for some retirees because the need for a higher death benefit is typically greatest in the early years of retirement. During the ten years of the term policy, Frank's assets are expected to grow, creating some "self-insurance" for the family. Also, Pam will be ten years older, and her remaining life expectancy will be shorter, in which case there may be less of a need for insurance. When the term expires, Frank will still have the permanent policy to meet their potentially lesser needs. Some universal life policies guarantee that both the death benefit and price will not change. Carefully research the policy and verify the length of time the policy is guaranteed. As an extra incentive, a few life insurance companies offer different variations of long-term care provisions as part of their policies. Using the survivor annuity dollars to also provide some long-term care support can be a nice added benefit while the insured is living. Keep in mind: these riders differ among companies.

Upon Frank's death, Pam will receive an income-tax-free death benefit. She can elect to create needed income in the form of an immediate annuity or a lump sum and invest it.

Frank and Pam also have two children and five grandchildren to whom they would like to leave an inheritance. Having a life insurance policy will help them meet this goal in two ways: First, if Pam does not use all of the death benefit, she can pass it on to her heirs. Secondly, if Pam predeceases Frank, he could name a secondary beneficiary, leaving the proceeds to his children.

A major factor in Pam and Frank's decision—as with most federal retirees—is health coverage. Pam is currently covered under Frank's health insurance (FEHB). He will need to select at least the minimum amount of survivor annuity for Pam to continue FEHB coverage if he were to pass away. Frank speaks with an insurance professional and decides that he will use a private policy to supplement his survivor benefit needs rather than take a full survivor benefit. However, he does select a recommended amount of survivor annuity benefit that will allow Pam to stay on his federal health insurance in the event that he dies before she does. This allows them to maximize their benefits and safety nets while minimizing costs.

Before filling out the paperwork and getting Pam's signature to change the survivor annuity, they should have the life insurance in place—and so should you! It's also important to make sure all premium payments are paid on time so that the policy does not lapse, leaving a surviving spouse with no benefits. We usually recommend that the covered survivor own the life insurance policy.

CLOSING THOUGHTS

This discussion has been based solely on survivor annuity options. There are many things to consider, and most people need an insurance professional to help them understand their options. The point of this chapter has been to educate you in the survivor benefit options available to you so that you can compare them to what you can obtain on the private market. You need to know your options in order to weigh them against each other.

Do not blindly accept the default survivor benefit. You are in control, not OPM. Your robust pension income will most likely be needed by your surviving spouse. Do your due diligence and be a wise consumer by knowing all of your options. Whether you pay for life insurance premiums, take the pension reduction that comes with survivor benefits, or both, know that it will not be cheap.

Lastly, we must point out that we have not thoroughly discussed covering the survivor's full need. Remember, the maximum annuity replacement amount is 55 percent for CSRS employees and 50 percent for FERS employees. Will this be sufficient to meet your beneficiary's needs? Will the amount be too much, and therefore a needless expense? You need to consult with an insurance professional to complete a needs analysis and find out. The choice is an individual but important one that many federal employees are not even aware of! You have options—it's up to you now to get the help you need to appropriately weigh them and make the right decision.

CHAPTER 5

Social Security—So Many Paths to Consider

AT RETIREMENT BENEFITS INSTITUTE, we frequently field questions from federal employees about Social Security. It is one of the most commonly discussed topics. *Will my Social Security be there for me? How much will I receive? Is it taxed? Will an earnings test apply to me? How do I maximize my benefits? Am I doing all I can to lighten my future tax burden? I am CSRS and do not pay into Social Security—will Social Security affect me? And what are these Government Pension Offset (GPO) and Windfall Elimination Provision (WEP) rules I keep hearing about?* These are the questions that federal employees need answered to ensure that they are maximizing not just their Social Security, but their entire retirement income.

If you are a FERS employee, pay special attention to this chapter, as Social Security is an important part of the three-legged stool that makes up your retirement income. (CSRS employees generally do not pay into or receive Social Security. *Generally.* More on this later in the chapter.)

The Social Security Administration gives you the option to start receiving retirement benefits as early as age sixty-two, or to delay them up to age seventy in order to receive higher benefits. The time at which you choose to start taking benefits can have a major impact on your retirement income. This is a choice that should not be made haphazardly. You want to maximize not just your Social Security, but also your entire benefits package. This is complicated—you have to understand Social Security benefits, and how taxation, retirement income, and other benefits interact with Social Security. Only then can you really plan and act accordingly regarding your Social Security benefits.

The front page of the 2014 Social Security statement reads: "Without changes, in 2033 the Social Security Trust Fund will be able to pay only about 77 cents for each dollar of scheduled benefits." We know the Social Security system will have to change, but we don't yet know how. The government will have to make some changes either to benefits or to the way the system is funded, or both.

Since the future of the Social Security system is unknown, we will discuss the current rules in place upon the publication of this book in 2015. (Consult the RBI website for updated information.) We don't know what will happen with Social Security in the future, but we can

http://retireinstitute.com/your -benefits/social-security/

safely assume that Congress will not scrap the entire program. You may not get what you were promised, but you will almost certainly receive some percentage of your benefits, which makes the current rules at least relevant, no matter your age.

Please note that one way the Social Security Administration (SSA) is cutting costs is by no longer annually mailing paper statements. To get your statements, you must now log in to the SSA website at: ssa.gov/myaccount.

ELIGIBILITY

To be eligible for Social Security benefits upon retirement, you must have earned forty credits. Employees can earn up to four credits per year. Generally speaking, FERS retirees will almost always have the necessary forty credits.

Once eligible, retirees may begin receiving reduced benefits as early as age sixty-two. By waiting until full retirement age (FRA), full benefits may be received. Please see the chart below to determine your FRA:

FULL RETIREMENT AGE	
Year of Birth*	Full Retirement Age
1943–1954	66
1955	66 and 2 months
1956	66 and 4 months
1957	66 and 6 months
1958	66 and 8 months
1959	66 and 10 months
1960 and later	67

*People who were born on January 1 of any year should refer to the previous year.

BENEFITS

The amount of your Social Security benefit will depend on two things: how much you've earned throughout your working career, and the age at which you apply for benefits. The highest thirty-five years of earnings are used to compute your full benefit. If you have not worked thirty-five years by the time you retire, there will be zeros in your average earnings.

You must wait until your full retirement age in order to receive your full Social Security benefit. The Early Retirement Benefits chart illustrates the percentage of benefit you can receive if you decide to draw Social Security before your full retirement age.

EARLY RETIREMENT BENEFITS		
Age of Application	Benefit if FRA = 66	Benefit if FRA = 67
62	75%	70%
63	80%	75%
64	86.7%	80%
65	93.3%	86.7%
66	100%	93.3%
67		100%

In addition to the option of drawing your benefit early, you have the choice to delay the receipt of your benefit. If you delay your benefit, it increases every year until age seventy, which is the latest you would want to delay taking your Social Security benefit. The Delayed Retirement Benefits chart illustrates how waiting to retire can increase your Social Security benefit by a defined percentage:

DELAYED RETIREMENT BENEFITS		
Apply at Age	If FRA = 66	If FRA = 67
66	100%	93.3%
67	108%	100%
68	116%	108%
69	124%	116%
70	132%	124%

SPOUSAL BENEFITS

Spousal Social Security benefits may be available to both current and former spouses. Spousal benefits generally may be drawn as early as age sixty-two, but the benefit will be reduced. If the benefit is drawn at full retirement age, the spousal benefit will be half of the primary worker's benefit amount. If drawn at age sixty-two, the benefit is reduced to 35 percent. For a former spouse to receive benefits, the marriage must have lasted at least ten years, and the person receiving the spousal benefits must be unmarried.

Sara is still employed by the federal government as a FERS employee. When she retires at her full retirement age, she will have two options from which to choose. The first option is to take her husband's spousal Social Security benefit. Her second option is to go with her own benefit, though she may be better served to delay taking her own benefit until she is seventy years old, at which point she will receive her maximum benefit.

If you're like us, you are thinking two things here: *How confusing!* and *No wonder the system is going broke!*

SURVIVOR BENEFITS

Social Security survivor benefits are available to current spouses who have been married for at least nine months at the date of death, except in the case of an accident. Former spouses are also eligible for survivor benefits as long as they were married for at least ten years. Survivor benefits are not available if the widow or widower remarries before age sixty, unless that marriage ends. Reduced benefits may be drawn as early as age sixty, but the survivor must wait until full retirement age to receive the full benefit.

Survivor benefits are also available for minor children up to age eighteen (or age nineteen if they are still attending secondary school full time). Benefits can be received at any age in cases where the child was disabled before the age of twenty-two and remains disabled.

— PLANNING TIP —

If a child receives this benefit, the federal survivor's monthly benefits will be reduced dollar for dollar. For example, if a child receives $200 per month in federal monthly benefits and $400 per month from Social Security, then his or her federal benefit will be reduced dollar for dollar, making the combined benefit from Social Security and federal survivor benefit only $400 per month, not $600. Be aware of this reduction when planning for your minor children's futures.

I AM NOT COVERED UNDER FERS—WILL SOCIAL SECURITY BENEFIT ME?

It depends, but generally not very much. Since CSRS employees do not contribute to Social Security, most CSRS employees will not be eligible for Social Security benefits unless they earned their forty credits in another job outside the federal government.

There are also specific situations in which a worker who has not paid into the Social Security system may still receive Social Security benefits through the Government Pension Offset (though this is quite rare).

WINDFALL ELIMINATION PROVISION (WEP)

CSRS, CSRS offset, and FERS transfer employees may be eligible to receive Social Security benefits despite having worked for some years without paying into the Social Security system. Don't get too excited though! There is a rule known as the Windfall Elimination Provision that can reduce such retirees' Social Security benefits. This rule generally affects only the aforementioned retirees because they have all or a portion of their annuity calculated based on time during which they were not actually paying into the Social Security system.

A small Social Security check could be roughly cut in half, but you will never see more than the maximum reduction ($413 per month in 2015, though this number can change each year). The blow can be cushioned if you have more than twenty years of *substantial earnings*, as defined by the Social Security Administration.

With thirty or more years of substantial earnings, the WEP is completely eliminated. It is more common to see CSRS offsets and FERS transfers with more than twenty years of substantial earnings than CSRS employees. Check your Social Security statement to determine if you have enough good years.

Visit the RBI website for annual updates and more information on WEP.

http://retireinstitute.com
/wep-changes/

GOVERNMENT PENSION OFFSET (GPO)

While CSRS employees typically do not receive Social Security benefits, they may be eligible—*in theory*—to receive a spousal Social Security benefit. However, GPO is another provision that can reduce Social Security spousal benefits received by CSRS retirees. If a CSRS retiree takes a spousal Social Security benefit, that benefit is reduced by two-thirds of the CSRS pension. In our experience, GPO generally eliminates the spousal benefit.

This provision affects only CSRS retirees. GPO does *not* apply to CSRS offsets.

This is an oft-overlooked potential loss of revenue. In the event of your spouse's passing, will you be able to live comfortably without that extra Social Security income? We recommend that you complete a needs analysis to be sure.

— Planning Tip —

Are you full retirement age for Social Security and still working? Consider drawing Social Security now, since you are not a pensioner, yet neither WEP nor GPO will apply!

MAXIMIZING YOUR BENEFIT

There are various strategies for maximizing your Social Security benefit. The most straightforward way is to improve the earnings record on which your benefit is based. The highest thirty-five years of earnings are used to calculate your benefit. If you have worked less than thirty-five years, you will have years with $0 averaged into your earnings record, in which case working longer can raise your benefit. Working longer can also raise your benefit if you earn more now than in previous years. Check your Social Security statement online to see if you have any years with $0 so you can verify its accuracy and see if working longer will improve your benefit.

Another way to maximize your benefit is by coordinating your Social Security benefit with your spouse's. There are nine filing options for people applying singly and an astounding eighty-one filing options for couples! Strategizing to determine which is the right option can substantially increase your benefits for life. We will briefly discuss two of the most common strategies.

One method is called *file and suspend*. In this strategy, the higher-earning spouse applies for benefits at full retirement age—and then asks for it to be suspended. This allows the lower-earning spouse to begin drawing the spousal benefit while also allowing the higher-earning spouse's benefit to continue growing until age seventy.

Another filing option is what we call "claim now, claim more later." For this strategy to work, the lower-earning spouse must have already filed for Social Security benefits. Once the higher-earning spouse reaches full retirement age, he or she elects to receive a spousal benefit based on the low earner's benefits, but not on his or her own benefits. Then, at age seventy, the higher-earning spouse switches to his or her own benefit, which has now had time to grow to the maximum amount.

Strategies such as these can be complex, and there are many rules that need to be considered to ensure maximum benefit. Given that there are so many options and permutations, we highly recommend seeking out a professional's advice when considering your Social Security benefit options.

WORKING IN RETIREMENT

Do you know what you call working in retirement? Anything but retirement! Retiring and then starting another job kind of defeats the purpose of retirement, right?

Jokes aside, while working in retirement may seem like an oxymoron, there are in fact many reasons why a federal retiree might continue to work after retiring from service. Some people do so for personal reasons, and others because they need the extra money in retirement. Whatever your reasons, you should understand how earning income in retirement can affect your Social Security benefits.

If you begin drawing Social Security before you reach your full retirement age (FRA), you will be subject to an annual earnings test that could reduce your benefit. For 2015, the annual earnings limit is $15,720. (This may change each year. For updated information, visit our website at retireinstitute.com.) For every two dollars you earn over this limit, one dollar of your Social Security benefit will be withheld. For example, if you earned $10,000, nothing would be withheld. However, if you earned $20,000, you would be $4,280 over the limit, and your benefit would be reduced by half of that, or by $2,140.

However, there is a three-for-one special in the year that you turn FRA. During this year the earnings limit states that for every three dollars you go over the limit, one dollar will be withheld. This will only last for the one year that you reach FRA; after that, the earnings limit test no longer applies.

Only *earned income* is used in this calculation—that is, money that you earn from working. You would normally receive a W-2 or 1099 for this income. Rest assured, your federal annuity, thrift savings plan (TSP) withdrawals, and investment incomes do *not* count toward this limit.

Once you reach your FRA, the earnings test disappears and you are free to earn as much as you like without worrying that it will have a negative effect on your Social Security benefit. In the meantime, don't let the earnings test stop you from working and making extra money if you need to. You can always delay the receipt of Social Security until your FRA or when you stop working, whichever comes first. Even if you are already receiving Social Security, it may still make sense to work in retirement despite the penalty.

SOCIAL SECURITY TAXATION—BEWARE *DOUBLE* TAXATION!

Just because you stop working does not mean you get to stop paying taxes. (If only it were so!) Depending on your combined income, a portion of your Social Security income may be subject to income tax. The table below outlines the tax structure for Social Security benefits as of 2015:

TAXES ON SOCIAL SECURITY		
Filing Status	**Provisional Income***	**Amount of SS Subject to Tax**
Married Filing Jointly	Under $32,000	0
	$32,000 – $44,000	Up to 50%
	Over $44,000	Up to 85%
Single, Head of Household, Qualifying Widower	Under $25,000	0
	$25,000 – $34,000	Up to 50%
	Over $34,000	Up to 85%
Married Filing Separately	Over $0	85%

Provisional Income = Modified Adjusted Gross Income + Half of Social Security Benefit + Tax-Exempt Interest

If you stay below the threshold for taxation, you will not see a tax on your Social Security. However, this is rare for federal employees due to their robust pensions. Your provisional income includes your household pension, any earned income from employment, taxable TSP or IRA withdrawals, other income items (dividends, interest, capital gains, rental property income, and other taxable income, etc.), *plus* half of Social Security. Here we see all three legs of the retirement income stool coming together to create a perfect storm of taxation. Most federal employees and their spouses will face Social Security taxation.

If you are married filing jointly and your provisional income is over $44,000, the government considers you *wealthy* and will tax up to 85 percent of your Social Security benefits. Suppose you retire and find yourself at that provisional income bubble of $44,000. Now suppose you want to have a big party, so you take one dollar from your traditional TSP, making your provisional income $44,001. Not only will you have to face taxation on this TSP withdrawal, but because your provisional income has gone above the threshold, it has also triggered tax on 85 percent of a Social Security dollar.

In effect, the withdrawal from the TSP triggers two taxes—the tax on the TSP dollar *and* a tax on your Social Security that you wouldn't have had to pay otherwise. If you are in the 15 percent bracket, you will face a 15 percent tax on that dollar as well as an additional 15 percent tax on 85 percent of a Social Security dollar. You will pay fifteen cents tax on the TSP dollar *and* thirteen cents for Social Security tax. In other words, every TSP dollar taken out triggers a twenty-eight-cent tax.

This is sometimes a difficult concept for people to grasp because the second tax isn't actually on the TSP withdrawal (it is on Social Security), though it is triggered by the TSP withdrawal.

Let's consider an example: Jerry and his wife, Denise, have a combined income of $44,000 from their pensions and half of Social Security. To supplement their income in retirement, they take $1,000 from Jerry's TSP. They only have to pay $150 in federal income tax on this $1,000, but they now also have to pay tax on $850 of their Social Security income that wasn't taxable before they drew from the TSP. They have taken one action that triggers two taxes—$150 from TSP and $130 from Social Security. I think we can all agree that $280 is a lot on a $1,000 withdrawal for someone in the 15 percent income tax bracket!

SO WHAT CAN YOU DO ABOUT IT?

Thankfully, there are several forward-looking strategies that can help you avoid this double tax. For starters, how about trying a Roth account? Unlike traditional TSP and IRA withdrawals, withdrawals from Roth funds (and the cash value of certain life insurance policies) do not generally create additional tax liability on your Social Security. This means that a Roth account may substantially lower your tax burden in retirement. (For more information on Roth accounts, see Chapter 7.)

Don't let taxes erode your income in retirement. You need to ask yourself whether you understand this double tax and its implications. Will you pay higher taxes in retirement than you do today? Are you saving funds in the right tax structure so as to avoid this "double tax" in retirement? If not, you need to get yourself to a professional who can explain how the three legs of the stool can combine to create this often avoidable "double tax."

WHEN SHOULD I APPLY?

Many FERS employees have trouble deciding when to start drawing Social Security benefits. *When* you apply will affect how large a benefit you will receive, but many people cannot wait until age seventy to start receiving Social Security just to maximize the benefit.

There are five major points to consider when making this decision: personal health, life expectancy, income needs, working after retirement, and survivor needs.

Many of these points of consideration have been discussed already, and others are self-explanatory. The five points are simple enough, but how they fit into your overall financial picture can be complex and confusing. For some people, all factors will point in the same direction, and the decision will be simple. Others will have to weigh the pros and cons more carefully to find the best strategy.

Are you doing everything you can to educate yourself about Social Security? Have you considered the earnings test? Are you aware of the double tax you may face on TSP withdrawals if you surpass the combined income threshold? Do you know when to start drawing Social Security benefits? Do you know when to draw your own versus your spouse's? These are critical matters that will affect your retirement income. Only careful planning and sound financial strategies will allow you to maximize your income. No single strategy is right for everyone, so be sure to know your options and seek out professional help.

CHAPTER 6

The Thrift Savings Plan Demystified

PERSONAL SAVINGS ARE an important part of the retirement picture for both FERS and CSRS employees. Most federal employees will not be able to meet all of their retirement income needs with their annuity alone. They will also draw substantially upon their savings.

Federal employees spend their entire working careers contributing to these savings in what we call the accumulation phase. Retirement marks the transition into the distribution phase, at which point they switch from making contributions to making withdrawals.

A sound retirement plan considers both the accumulation and distribution phases. You have spent your working life saving, and you are finishing strong. It is now time to make sure you understand how your retirement accounts function in the distribution phase so that you can maximize your income streams as you begin making withdrawals on your savings.

WHAT IS THE THRIFT SAVINGS PLAN?

Many federal employees spend the accumulation phase contributing to the Thrift Savings Plan (TSP), which is a tax-advantaged 401(k)-type program offered by the federal government. Contributions made to a traditional TSP are not subject to income tax until they are withdrawn ("tax me later"), while contributions to a Roth TSP are taxed up front ("tax me now"), but generally no tax will be due upon withdrawal. Both CSRS and FERS employees are eligible to participate in the TSP, though different conditions and incentives apply. The TSP has the same contribution limits as other 401(k) plans. In 2015, employees may contribute $18,000, and employees age fifty or older can contribute an extra $6,000 for a total of $24,000. These amounts can change from year to year. Consult the Retirement Benefits Institute website for the latest numbers.

http://retireinstitute.com/your-benefits/roth-tsp-ira/

FERS AND TSP—FREE MONEY!

The federal government will match TSP contributions made by FERS employees up to 5 percent of their salary. The TSP match is handled differently than most employer matches. The government contributes 1 percent of your salary to your TSP account, even if you yourself do not contribute anything. To get the additional 4 percent government contribution, you must contribute 5 percent of your salary. CSRS employees do not receive an employer match.

Don't leave free money on the table! Contribute enough to receive your full match or you are passing up free money.

— PLANNING TIP —

The employer match is contributed every pay period, not annually. Be sure to spread your TSP contributions evenly throughout the year.

Some people make all of their contributions early in the year, giving themselves extra cash flow for Christmas. Others try to put the money in at the beginning of the year to maximize potential investment returns, and others simply put off making contributions until the end of the year out of negligence. These are all major mistakes that will cost you part of your employer match for pay periods in which you did not contribute the required 5 percent of your salary. This is failing to collect free money— don't do it!

TSP FUND CHOICES

Like all tax-advantaged investment vehicles, the TSP is designed to hold your investment portfolio. The TSP has five funds from which to choose. They are described in the following chart:

TSP INDIVIDUAL FUNDS		
Regular Funds	**Description**	**Index**
G Fund	Government Securities	
F Fund	Mix of government and corporate bonds	Barclays Capital U.S. Aggregate Bond Index
C Fund	Large-cap U.S. stocks	Standard & Poor's 500 (S&P 500)
S Fund	Mix of small- and mid-cap U.S. stocks	Dow Jones U.S. Completion Total Stock Market Index
I Fund	Mostly large-cap foreign stocks	Morgan Stanley Capital International EAFE (Europe, Australasia, Far East) Index

L FUNDS: THE BLENDED CHOICE

In addition to these individual funds, you may also invest in Lifecycle (L) Funds, which are predetermined combinations of all five regular funds. The L Funds are designed to automatically shift into a more conservative, lower-risk portfolio allocation as you approach your target date. This makes it easier for you to stay invested aggressively while you're younger and dial back your exposure to risk as you near retirement. Each quarter, the target asset allocations in L Funds change, shifting toward a less risky mix of investments.

In order to pick an L Fund, decide when you expect to begin withdrawing the money from your TSP account. Select the L Fund that best matches your target date. Consult the following chart, provided by the Federal Retirement Thrift Investment board at the tsp.gov website for reference:

Choose:	IF YOUR TARGET DATE IS:
L 2050	2045 or later
L 2040	2035 through 2044
L 2030	2025 through 2034
L 2020	2015 through 2024
L Income	If you are already withdrawing your account in monthly payments or expect to begin withdrawing in 2015

Your portfolio can contain more than one L Fund or a combination of L Funds and individual funds, if you so choose.

Picking an L Fund is generally a better strategy than not having any investment strategy, as it provides some intentional diversification of asset classes and rebalancing. It can make investing and staying diversified easier. However, the question for you is, while L Funds may be easier, is it the best thing to do to maximize your retirement income?

You shouldn't be making investment decisions based on what is easiest or what the government suggests that you do. You should be invested in what gives you the right combination of risk and returns.

There are services in the financial marketplace that can professionally manage your TSP for you, making appropriate allocations and trades based on your plans and goals rather than letting the L Fund do it automatically. Contact us if you would like to explore such programs.

WITHDRAWALS WHILE WORKING

Withdrawals made from your TSP while you're still employed are considered in-service withdrawals. There are three types of in-service withdrawals.

The first type is actually a loan and is not technically considered a withdrawal as long as it is paid back. If the loan is not repaid by the time you retire, it will be considered a distribution and you will owe tax on the remaining balance. You may still contribute to the TSP while you are repaying your loan. Some employees take loans from their TSP to cover unexpected or major expenses because the interest rate for these loans is typically quite low, close to the G Fund rate of return.

The second type of in-service TSP withdrawal is the financial hardship withdrawal, which is not a loan and does not have to be repaid. These withdrawals can be taken at any age, but you must prove financial hardship first. There are downsides to making this kind of withdrawal. You will owe taxes on the money and possibly an early withdrawal penalty if the withdrawal is taken before you reach age fifty-nine and a half. You are also not allowed to contribute to your TSP for six months following this kind of distribution.

The last type of in-service withdrawal is the age-based withdrawal. This type of withdrawal is a one-time-only option that you may exercise once you reach age fifty-nine and a half. This is a useful type of withdrawal because it allows you to take your money out of the TSP and put it into another type of account. Many people take the distribution and roll it into an IRA and/ or a Roth IRA, often to allow for more control over their money.

The most common reasons people give for rolling out of the TSP are:

- They are unsure how to manage their TSP and want professional help.
- They want to be more proactive with tax planning; they need more choices and more control over when and how they withdraw funds in retirement (more to come on the restrictiveness of TSP withdrawals).
- They have access to more investment options.

Many people worry that rolling over the TSP into an IRA will cause a tax burden. Rest assured that this is not the case. *Properly* rolling your traditional TSP into a traditional IRA will not create a taxable event. Please consult a professional to make sure this is done correctly.

Even after taking an early withdrawal and rolling your TSP into an IRA, you may still continue to contribute to the TSP for the remainder of your career. Making this type of early withdrawal can be a good strategy for some people, but it can also limit your ability to make another withdrawal later (as we discuss in the next section), so you should be strategic about when to make any withdrawals from your TSP.

WITHDRAWALS IN RETIREMENT

Retirement requires you to shift your thinking. After accumulating savings in the TSP for a whole working career, it can be frightening and difficult to transition into the withdrawal stage. But remember, you socked away all those savings so that you could use them in retirement—not so that you could be the richest person in the cemetery. Enjoy your retirement savings in this new stage of life.

There are limited options for withdrawals from your TSP. You may leave all of your funds in the TSP, but you must start taking required minimum distributions (RMDs) from your TSP starting no later than April 1 of the year following the year in which you turn seventy and a half. You must continue to do this for the rest of retirement.

What if you forget to take the RMD? Well, I will leave you to understand the forfeiture rules of your account by reading TSP-775. They are long and complex, but rest assured, *forfeiture is not what you want to happen.*

You are allowed to take a one-time partial withdrawal from your TSP in retirement. However, you are not eligible for this if you already took the age-based withdrawal while working. After this one-time partial withdrawal, the TSP will not allow you to treat it like a bank. The TSP will remain in control, only giving you the full withdrawal option.

This can limit your options when it comes to withdrawing funds. The only other option besides the one-time partial withdrawal is to take a full withdrawal, and there are four different ways to do this:

- You may take it all in a single payment.
- You can receive it in monthly payments.
- You can transfer it to an IRA, 401(k), or other similar account.
- You may opt to have it converted into a life annuity.

You may also do some combination of all of the above when taking a full withdrawal.

Generally, there is a mandatory federal tax withholding of 20 percent for any funds you receive directly from the TSP. You may find that you end up owing more or less when you actually file your tax return.

— PLANNING TIP —

IRAs give you the power to withhold as much or as little as you see fit, allowing you greater control over your money. The ability to control the tax withholding from distributions can potentially save you real tax dollars. This is one more reason to consider an IRA.

Bottom line: The TSP is great for accumulation, but it limits your distribution options. Many retirees choose to roll funds to IRAs for this reason.

Please check our online video for a deeper look at these choices, and to see examples of how the full withdrawal option can work for you.

http://retireinstitute.com/resources/videos/

THE TSP HAS ITS USES!

While there are advantages to rolling your TSP into an IRA, it is also true that the TSP runs a low-cost platform. If you move to a private account, your fees will most likely be higher, but the added flexibility can be worth the cost. A common strategy is to use the TSP in the accumulation phase and then roll the money into an IRA during the distribution phase so that you can take advantage of the TSP's low cost but still utilize the IRA's flexibility.

Use both accounts in such a way as to maximize their advantages and minimize their disadvantages.

— PLANNING TIP —

When running a cost-benefit analysis of a private account versus the TSP, make sure you are comparing after-fee historical returns on the private account to the TSP net returns. There are funds and strategies that have historically had stronger track records than the TSP. However, you want to be sure that fees don't cost you more than you are gaining by using a private account.

TRADING IN YOUR TSP FOR AN IMMEDIATE ANNUITY— DOES IT MAKE SENSE?

Converting your TSP into an immediate annuity with a fixed payment made to the annuitant for the term of the contract is a possibility. However, immediate annuities are the least-commonly used option due to the complexity and inflexibility of the annuity choices. At the time of the writing of this book, there are eighteen options from which to choose.

In the simplest of terms, choosing an immediate annuity means exchanging your lump sum for an income stream. There are pros and cons involved with this.

The positive aspect of taking an annuity is that you secure a guaranteed income stream for yourself and possibly your spouse for as long as one of you lives. In simple terms, you are buying a sense of safety from the provider.

The downside of buying an immediate annuity is that you typically do not get increases that can keep pace with inflation. Also, if you annuitize the traditional TSP, you will pay tax on every withdrawal *forever*.

Be careful in making such a selection. You lose all control as you battle your two enemies in retirement: taxes and inflation (more on this in Chapter 8).

ALERT: SPECIAL PRIVILEGES FOR FIFTY-FIVE-YEAR-OLDS!

If you retire in the year you turn fifty-five or later, you can withdraw from your TSP without being subject to the 10 percent early withdrawal penalty. You may recall that for IRAs you must be at least fifty-nine and a half to avoid the 10 percent penalty. If you plan to retire and expect to use a portion of your TSP before age fifty-nine and a half, you should not immediately transfer your whole TSP to an IRA. Doing so will result in an unnecessary penalty if you need to withdraw funds. You must first determine how much money you will need from your TSP during the time between retirement and age fifty-nine and a half. This much money should be left in the TSP for monthly withdrawal, while the remainder can be transferred into an IRA.

CALL TO ACTION

As you can see, there are many useful strategies you can employ to maximize your savings. You should not leave your money in a TSP just because it's the easiest route. Make sure you know all of your options and the consequences of the planning choices you make, as well as the ones that you *could* make.

To learn even more about TSP, please visit the Retirement Benefits Institute website and consult our online training materials. You have many options at your disposal for managing personal savings. It is not enough just to contribute to these programs. You need to contribute to the right types of accounts, in the right amount, and at the right times in order to reduce your tax burden, maximize your assets, and enjoy an optimal retirement income.

http://retireinstitute.com/your
-benefits/tsp-investments/

Chapter 7

Roth Accounts and the Voluntary Contribution Program

THE PREVIOUS CHAPTER focuses on the Thrift Savings Plan (TSP). This chapter will delve deeper into Roth TSPs and Roth IRAs. We will also share advanced tax strategies for funding these unique accounts in a way that maximizes the reduction in your future tax burden while allowing for the financial control you need in retirement.

It's important to understand that a Roth, like a traditional TSP or IRA, is not itself an investment, but rather a tax "wrapper" (or "bucket") to hold different investments of your choosing. Inside this wrapper you may have stocks, bonds, mutual funds, annuities, real estate, and so on. We will not discuss the investments in this chapter, but we will go into detail about the "wrapper."

Federal employees typically have two kinds of Roth accounts available to them: the Roth TSP and the Roth IRA. Each share the same basic qualities that define a Roth account, but they follow different sets of rules that offer different sets of advantages and disadvantages. The first part of this chapter will delve into the intricacies and the pros and cons of each.

THE NEW KID ON THE BLOCK: ROTH TSP

In 2012, a Roth feature was rolled out. This new feature allows employees to contribute to a traditional TSP, a Roth TSP, or both.

Today, the vast majority of TSP funds are still held in traditional TSP accounts, which are the "tax-me-later" type of tax-advantaged accounts. You do not pay taxes on income when you put it into a traditional TSP. However, you *do* pay taxes on any distributions from a traditional TSP.

This is the exact opposite of how a Roth TSP works. Funds contributed to the Roth account are made after tax, meaning you pay income taxes before the money goes into the retirement account. We call these "tax-me-now" savings accounts. You pay the taxes up front when you make contributions and do not have to pay tax on *any* distributions, as long as certain qualifications are met. Typically, investment earnings are tax-free, which make them a great opportunity to grow your retirement nest egg.

Contributing to the Roth TSP is easy, and the option to do so is open to all federal employees. There are no income limits for participation in a Roth TSP like there are with Roth IRAs. The contribution limit for Roth TSP is the same as for other 401(k)s. For this year's limits and further explanation of how Roth accounts work, please see our video on Roth accounts. You may choose to put half of your

http://retireinstitute.com
/resources/videos/

funds in Roth and half in traditional, or any other combination that suits your needs, but the contribution limit applies to the total of all contributions going into the TSP.

Under the current TSP rules, you are not allowed to convert existing TSP funds to a Roth TSP.

There are catches to the Roth TSP that can make them inflexible. All TSP withdrawals are subject to the "pro rata rule" that dictates *where* your withdrawals must come from. When you take withdrawals from your TSP, the pro rata rule requires you to draw from your traditional and Roth TSP accounts proportionately. For example, if you have 80 percent of your TSP in a traditional account and 20 percent in a Roth TSP, then twenty cents of every dollar you take from the TSP will be Roth; the other eighty cents will come from the taxable bucket. The pro rata rules limit your control over your distribution planning.

Roth TSPs are also subject to required minimum distributions (RMDs) after the age of seventy and a half, which can force you to take money out that you may not need.

— PLANNING TIP —

One of the primary advantages of a Roth in income planning is that it enables you to control the timing of tax-advantaged withdrawals. Unfortunately, when your Roth remains under the control of TSP in retirement, you lose flexibility and control due to restrictions and stipulations set out by TSP, such as the pro rata rule and RMDs.

However, if you roll the Roth TSP funds into a separate Roth IRA, you no longer have to contend with the pro rata rules or RMDs. This may give you greater control over the distribution of your savings. There are also other ways that a Roth IRA can sometimes offer greater control and flexibility. Read on to see what the IRA may be able to do for you.

ROTH IRA

The Roth TSP is not the only "tax-me-now" option at your disposal—there is also the Roth IRA. Although the Roth IRA and Roth TSP function similarly for tax purposes, the Roth IRA is governed by IRS Publication 590, which applies a different set of rules than the Employee Retirement Income Security Act (ERISA) rules that govern the Roth TSP. Thus, the contribution and distribution rules for the two types of Roth accounts are different.

For many federal employees, there are advantages to a Roth IRA. Like all Roth accounts, they offer tax-free growth and distribution, if certain requirements are met. Generally, you must be fifty-nine and a half years old and have held the account for at least five years before you can take distributions without paying tax or penalty on *the gain*.

Another advantage of the Roth IRA is that it allows you access to the basis (your contributions to the account) immediately without penalty or further tax. The Roth TSP only allows for withdrawals as described in the previous section. Access to the basis without penalty can be important if you need funds for any reason. If you suffer a medical emergency, need to make a major purchase, have to pay for your children's tuition, or have any other emergency need for cash, you can draw from your Roth IRA basis without tax or penalty. You don't have to wait five years to avoid a penalty or further tax as long as you draw the basis *only*, not the gain. (For some, this can actually be an alternative way to pay for tuition, rather than a 529 plan.)

Also, Roth IRAs do not restrict investment choices as the Roth TSP does. Furthermore, as previously mentioned, Roth IRAs are not subject to RMDs such as those seen with the Roth TSP. That makes Roth IRAs a great option for people who may not need to withdraw funds from their Roth account every year. For this reason, Roth IRAs are also an excellent choice for legacy planning. They make a wonderful vehicle for leaving an inheritance to your family. It's important to note that RMDs will be required of your non-spouse Roth IRA beneficiaries once they inherit the account, but generally it is *all* tax-free!

The Roth IRA can also serve as a solution to the inflexibility caused by the Roth TSP's pro rata rule. By choosing a Roth IRA over a Roth TSP, or by rolling your Roth TSP into a Roth IRA before you make any distributions, you can avoid the pro rata rules. This gives you greater control over your distribution planning.

Unfortunately, contribution limits for Roth IRAs are much lower than those for TSP. In 2015, Roth IRA contribution limits are $5,500, or $6,500 for those age fifty and older, whereas Roth

TSP contribution limits are $18,000, or $24,000 for those age fifty or older.

Roth IRAs also have income limits restricting those who can contribute—if you earn more than the limit, you cannot make contributions. Roth IRA contributions are subject to contribution phase-out for higher-earning individuals. According to the rules for 2015, single people earning more than $116,000 and married couples filing jointly who earn more than $183,000 are not able to contribute to a Roth IRA at all. (These limits are indexed to inflation and tend to go up every year. Consult the RBI website for current figures.) There are no such restrictions for the Roth TSP.

http://retireinstitute.com
/your-benefits/roth-tsp-ira/

The income and contributions limits won't necessarily preclude you from creating a sizeable Roth IRA if you can employ strategies for rolling money into it, which we will discuss in this chapter. Many people roll their Roth TSP into a Roth IRA upon retirement, or at age fifty-nine and a half, when they are eligible for a one-time age-based withdrawal from their TSP.

Bottom line: What makes the Roth IRA attractive to many people? The multiple ways in which it can provide greater control and flexibility over tax-advantaged savings. There is no reason not to investigate what a Roth IRA could do for you.

YOUR TAXES IN RETIREMENT

One of the primary differences between a Roth and a traditional account is *when* you pay taxes on it—at the time of contribution (Roth) or at the time of distribution (traditional). The conventional wisdom is that you should defer taxes until later, which would suggest that a traditional account is superior to a Roth. The reasoning behind this advice is that it assumes most people will fall into a lower marginal tax bracket after retirement.

It is true that many Americans may be able to pay less in federal tax by choosing a "tax-me-later" account, such as a traditional IRA or 401(k). But does this usually hold true for people who work for the federal government?

As it turns out, the conventional wisdom is often incorrect for federal employees because it does not consider their robust pensions. We have found that it is very common for federal employees to remain in the same marginal tax rate before and after retirement.

For example, many federal employees are currently in the top 25 percent bracket for taxable income (please note that this is line 43 of federal tax form 1040, after your deductions and exemptions, traditional TSP contributions, and health insurance premiums). In retirement, we find that many individuals simply end up at the bottom of this 25 percent bracket—not down in the 15 percent bracket. When they begin withdrawing funds from the TSP, they end up paying the same tax rate they would have paid while employed, negating most of the advantages of a traditional TSP. The charts on page 122 detail the 2015 tax brackets (these are subject to change each year).

For an example of how this works, consider the situation of two hypothetical retirees, Ralph and Wanda. Ralph has worked in private industry his entire life. Wanda is a FERS employee. Together, they have $146,000 of taxable income as they near retirement. Consulting the tax chart above, you'll find that this income puts them near the top of the 25 percent tax bracket. This is pretty typical for dual-income middle-class families. They have been told that they will fall into a lower tax bracket in retirement, which will make "tax-me-later" retirement accounts like the traditional TSP a better deal than the "tax-me-now" type. But will they really fall into a lower tax bracket? Not always, and in our experience, not even usually.

Let's run a possible scenario. Both receive Social Security, and Wanda has her FERS pension. Just these three basic income sources generate $80,000 of taxable income. At this level of income, which is not out of the ordinary for federal retirees, their TSP and 401(k) withdrawals will be taxed at the same 25 percent rate they were hoping to avoid at this stage in life. Examine the chart above to see the shift in their income and how it would relate to the 2015 tax brackets. (Note: The numbers in the chart will change every year, as the brackets are adjusted for inflation each year.)

In this scenario, the traditional TSP confers no greater tax advantage than the Roth TSP and Roth IRA. This makes all the other advantages of a Roth that we have outlined in this chapter look even better! If this situation is similar to your own—and as a federal employee with a pension it may well be—then you should strongly consider the advantages of a Roth.

Let's now look at a few other scenarios involving Ralph and Wanda to observe the differences between contributing to a Roth and contributing to a traditional TSP. Assume the same facts and figures stated earlier apply in both of the following scenarios. Let's also assume that Wanda has a beginning balance of $150,000 in her traditional TSP. She is now deciding whether she should continue contributing to the traditional TSP or start making contributions to a Roth TSP instead. It's 2015, and they plan to retire in 2023.

First, let's consider what would happen if they continue to make 10 percent contributions to the traditional TSP. This is shown in the chart on the following page:

TRADITIONAL TSP OPTION*	
Case Study: Continue to only contribute to the traditional TSP, 10 percent of pay with 5 percent FERS match.	
	Traditional TSP
2015	$167,700
2016	$186,108
2017	$205,252
2018	$225,162
2019	$245,868
2020	$267,403
2021	$289,799
2022	$313,091
2023	$337,315
After Tax Total:	$252,986

*Assumptions:
Salary in 2015: $75,000
Pay Increase: 2 percent
Rate of Return: 4 percent
Tax Rate: 25 percent
Beginning TSP Balance: $150,000

If we assume conservative growth in the TSP and a 25 percent tax on all distributions over multiple years, we get a net amount of $252,986 from the TSP. Not too bad!

Now let's see what would happen if Wanda were to switch contributions to the Roth TSP. Because they have to pay taxes on Roth contributions, this time they're making only a 7.5 percent post-tax contribution to the Roth TSP (functionally equivalent to the 10 percent pretax dollars from the previous example). They still have their 5 percent FERS employer-matching contribution going into the traditional TSP. This scenario is shown in the following chart:

TSP ROTH OPTION*		
Case Study: Stop contributing to traditional TSP, contribute 7.5 percent of pay (equivalent to 10 percent pretax) to Roth TSP with 5 percent FERS match going to the traditional account.		
	Traditional TSP	**Roth TSP**
2015	$159,900	$5,850
2016	$170,196	$11,934
2017	$180,903	$18,261
2018	$192,039	$24,841
2019	$203,621	$31,685
2020	$215,666	$38,802
2021	$228,193	$46,205
2022	$241,220	$53,903
2023	$254,769	$61,909
Total After Tax: $252,986		

*Assumptions:
Salary in 2015: $75,000
Pay Increase: 2 percent
Rate of Return: 4 percent
Tax Rate: 25 percent
Beginning Traditional TSP Balance: $150,000
Beginning Roth TSP Balance: $0

Note that in this scenario, the total after taxes is exactly the same. But the biggest difference is that Wanda has added a Roth bucket that will allow for *tax-free distributions in retirement*. Year by year, this diversification, paired with properly managed withdrawals, will generally add real dollars to her long-term retirement income stream.

This example illustrates that, in some cases, there is no advantage to putting your money into a "tax-me-later" account. Again, this is commonly true for federal employees who will receive a sizeable annuity.

If you will not experience a tax savings by dropping into a lower tax bracket in retirement, you should strongly consider the advantages of a Roth account. Ralph and Wanda might be well served to put their money into a Roth TSP and then roll it into a Roth IRA. This would enable them to enjoy the tax advantages of a Roth and gain greater control over their distributions.

A final potential advantage of the Roth, which is rarely talked about, is that it hedges you against the greatest unknown—what if federal tax rates go up? Tax rates are currently at historic lows. If tax rates go up in the future, you will be glad you put your money in a Roth and paid your taxes in advance.

TO ROTH OR NOT TO ROTH?

The decision to fund a Roth account instead of a traditional tax-advantaged account is an important one. When weighing your options, consider these three questions:

ARE YOU PLANNING TO RETIRE YOUNG?

Federal employees who plan to retire at a younger age, as many Special Provisions employees do, may want to fund a Roth IRA because these accounts give you access to tax-free cash earlier. You can roll your Roth TSP into a Roth IRA and access your basis. Remember the previously mentioned pro rata rules, which will still apply to your TSP accounts. Special Provisions employees should visit the Retirement Benefits Institute website for case studies.

http://retireinstitute.com
/special-provisions/

WILL REQUIRED MINIMUM DISTRIBUTIONS FORCE YOU TO TAKE MONEY YOU DON'T NEED?

You cannot park your money in the TSP or a traditional IRA forever. These accounts force you to take required minimum distributions (RMDs). Even your Roth TSP has RMDs that apply when you reach seventy and a half years of age. The first-year RMD requirement is about 3.7 percent of your total TSP and IRA balances. Failing to take your full RMD will result in a penalty of 50 percent of the amount that you should have withdrawn, plus the tax bill.

If you do not actually need this money but are forced to make an RMD anyway, you will have no choice but to place the funds into taxable accounts. Doing this may force you to start paying taxes on the earnings each year.

If you will have sufficient retirement income without having to withdraw funds from your TSP, you should consider a Roth IRA in order to avoid RMDs. This way you can avoid paying taxes on unneeded withdrawals, remain in control of your tax-bracket planning, and avoid withdrawing assets you might prefer to leave to your surviving spouse, as a legacy for your heirs, or to other charitable causes.

DO YOU HAVE A LONG WINDOW OF TIME BEFORE YOU WILL START TAKING DISTRIBUTIONS FROM YOUR RETIREMENT ACCOUNTS?

You should consider both your current and future tax brackets, as well as what potential effects Social Security taxation will have in the future. Those who feel their taxes will not be lower in retirement should look seriously at the advantages of a Roth. If your tax bracket is the same in retirement as it is now, you will pay less tax on a Roth account than a traditional account if the account grows in value (and we always hope our savings accounts do!) because Roth accounts shield your investment earnings from taxation. Allowing your money to grow in a tax-free vehicle over a long period of time can create substantial wealth.

In short, federal employees should strongly consider a Roth unless they have specific reasons not to, such as confirmation that their tax bracket really will be lower in retirement.

The rules governing Roth accounts are complex. You must meet various requirements in order to be sure that your withdrawals and gains are tax- and penalty-free. We encourage you to reach out to us on our website at retireinstitute.com, or in person, to talk about your own situation.

http://retireinstitute.com/

YOU MAKE TOO MUCH MONEY FOR A ROTH IRA—NOW WHAT?

You may still be able to open a Roth IRA—it will just take a few more steps to get there. The previously discussed income limit applies only to contributions, not conversions. Under current law, you may convert existing IRA funds to a Roth IRA regardless of your income.

When funds from a traditional IRA (on which you have not yet paid taxes) are converted to a Roth IRA, you will owe taxes on the amount converted. You should consult a tax professional to help you strategize timing and conversion amounts to plan for your tax bracket.

THE BIGGEST OPPORTUNITY YOU'VE NEVER HEARD OF: VOLUNTARY CONTRIBUTION PROGRAM TO ROTH

The rest of this chapter applies only to CSRS and CSRS offset employees.

Contributing to a Roth can lead to substantial tax savings later in life once your money has spent considerable time growing in a tax-free environment. A large Roth account is an enviable goal. Normally, this dream can only be realized by making years of steady contributions, but for CSRS and CSRS offset employees who take advantage of the Voluntary Contribution Program (VCP), the dream of creating a large Roth account could quickly become a reality.

Let us stress that this strategy has *huge* implications. The VCP allows CSRS employees to create a Roth IRA worth several hundred thousand dollars. CSRS employees may be able to use the VCP to turn after-tax funds into a Roth IRA worth up to 10 percent of their lifetime federal earnings with very few tax implications!

The VCP was originally established as an additional savings account that would supplement and increase retirement annuities. Not many people knew about or participated in the VCP when the program was introduced because it provided very few perceived advantages to the retiree. However, the Pension Protection Act of 2006 created a unique opportunity for qualified employees to fund a large Roth IRA via the VCP quickly, and without incurring a large tax bill.

This is a multistep process, and we strongly recommend working with a financial professional who has experience using the VCP. Such a professional will help ensure that you get through the process quickly and effectively. This must be done right.

For this to work, any service deposits or redeposits that you owe must be paid before you fund your VCP. As discussed in Chapter 2, these deposits are typical of employees who have performed temporary or seasonal work at some time during their careers or have had a break in service along the way. Check with your human resources department to determine if you have any outstanding deposits or redeposits.

Next, you need to submit a simple form to open your VCP account. It may take several weeks to receive your account number in the mail. Once it is open, you may then begin funding your account.

You will use after-tax money to fund your VCP. Available assets can be in the form of cash, CDs, mutual funds, bonds, etc. Note that you should *not* use TSP, IRA, or Roth funds for this transaction. Most people prefer to fund their VCP online using pay.gov. This online system is simple and allows you to make your contributions electronically. You may deposit funds directly from your bank account or by using your credit card. Using your credit card (and of course paying it off with cash you have on hand) may even allow you to earn extras from your credit card company, such as airline miles or cash-back rewards. Yes, we have known CSRS employees who have run over $200,000 through their credit cards, getting the extra rewards just for using the card! We recommend a test run with your card to make sure this works for you before attempting it on a large scale.

Upon funding your VCP, you will take a refund of the contributions by modifying a distribution form and sending the form to your pre-established Roth IRA. You'll then have quickly funded a Roth IRA without having to pay substantial taxes! The only taxes that you'll owe from this process are on the small amount of earnings made while the funds sat inside the VCP, which the illustration on the following page depicts:

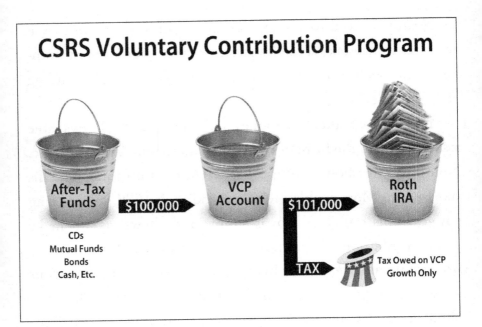

Please note that you should take the refund from the VCP before final adjudication of your retirement annuity. This is very important! If this step is not taken before your final adjudication, the funds in your VCP will be treated as an additional annuity and you will not be able to create your Roth IRA. For this reason, we recommend having the refund completed *before* submitting your retirement application.

Used in this way, the VCP is an amazing vehicle for creating a large Roth account, but doing so requires advanced knowledge of many federal programs. For more clarity on the matter, visit our website and be sure to check out the video.

http://retireinstitute.com
/vcp-voluntary-contributions/

FINDING A RETIREMENT PROFESSIONAL

This chapter is intended to give you a greater understanding of Roth accounts, and the VCP as a means to fund a Roth IRA. The Roth and the advanced planning strategies outlined in this chapter may not be right for everyone, but they will be right for many. The Roth, particularly the Roth IRA, has features that can afford you greater control of your tax future and greater control over your assets throughout your working life and all the way through retirement.

The tax code often dictates our behavior. Your goal should be to move as much of your assets as possible from a taxable state into a tax-free or tax-advantaged state. If you have hundreds of thousands of dollars of assets in taxable accounts, why wouldn't you move them into accounts that reduce your tax burden? Failing to do so can mean paying more in taxes than you actually have to.

Most people already have the majority of their funds in a "tax-me-later" bucket. If you are inspired to consider tax-strategy diversification, then we have pointed you in the right direction. Are you saving and planning to that end now? Even if you are retiring soon, it is not too late. You still have twenty to thirty years to grow your savings and withdraw your retirement funds. Plan accordingly. Plan for the long haul.

In this chapter and the previous one, we have tried to be thorough in offering advice on how to minimize your tax load on retirement savings. However, a volume this slim cannot possibly serve as a comprehensive guide that covers everyone's unique financial situations.

Now that you know the basics, this would be a good time to explore your options further by seeking out a retirement professional to help you understand whether a Roth is right for you and how it could best fit into your income plan. You're investing in your future here. You owe it to yourself to properly consider what the transition to a Roth TSP or a Roth IRA could mean for your future. Picking the right combination of retirement accounts is crucial to finding the best strategy for reducing your tax burden.

We work with many federal employees. We tell them all the same thing: Educate yourself! You need to look into Roth accounts and determine whether they are right or wrong for you. Don't blindly keep doing what you are doing now. Likewise, don't just automatically do what I outline in this chapter. Find out what is right for *you*.

CHAPTER 8

Minimizing the Impact of Taxes and Inflation in Retirement

TAXES AND INFLATION are the two main obstacles you will encounter along the path to a comfortable retirement. Making your money last means overcoming both.

Ask yourself: *Do I have the right investment and tax strategies in place to offset these ongoing threats?*

INFLATION IN RETIREMENT

We don't know what inflation will be in the future, but we believe there is good reason to be concerned. By the end of 2014, the national debt had surpassed $18 trillion, a number so large it is unfathomable for most people.[1] Worse, the national debt is still growing as the federal government continues to borrow more and more money. The rising debt is reaching crisis levels.

The federal government has historically dealt with rising debt in two main ways: by raising taxes and by printing money in

---

1 "U.S. Passes $18 Trillion in Debt, and Nothing's Being Done about It." PBS. n.d. Web. 26 Feb. 2015.

order to inflate it away. So far, it appears the government has mostly chosen the latter approach, borrowing and printing more and more money.

Inflation is not hard to see, and it accumulates surprisingly quickly over time. With people living longer, many retirements are now thirty years or more. Think back to what a postage stamp cost thirty years ago—only twenty cents. It's now almost a half dollar. That's an increase of 150 percent! This is happening across almost all consumer items.

We have actually been in a relatively low inflationary period for the last ten years or so. With the national debt rising and other pressures on the dollar, can inflation remain low through your retirement years? There is reason to doubt it.

Inflation can have sudden effects on retirees' purchasing power, especially if it starts at the beginning of their retirement. People retiring in the last high inflationary period of the late 1970s and early 1980s typically saw their buying power cut in half in just a few short years. If you don't plan for this contingency, such inflationary pressures could derail your retirement.

Don't let this happen to you. If the same thing occurs again, you need to have a plan already in place.

As a federal retiree, you will have one major advantage over many other retirees—your pension. Your monthly annuity will always be there. However, inflation can chip away at that annuity. Thankfully, FERS and CSRS retirees usually receive annual cost-of-living adjustments (COLAs) every year, which can help you keep pace with inflation.

WARNING: DO NOT EXPECT YOUR COLAS TO FULLY KEEP PACE WITH INFLATION

Historically speaking, the COLAs offered to federal employees for the past ten years have averaged between 1.97 percent (FERS) and 2.4 percent (CSRS). Over the last thirty years, however, inflation in the United States has averaged approximately 4.3 percent.[2] Health care costs are accelerating even faster. So, even in periods of low inflation, you can only count on your COLA to offset a portion of the historical inflation rate.

This means that you still need a plan in place to handle inflation not offset by your COLAs. Make sure that your investment and tax structures are set up to make up the difference. At Retirement Benefits Institute, we point federal employees toward professionals who can help with this planning. We would be honored to help you too.

FUTURE TAX RATES: WHAT WE DO AND DON'T KNOW

The rest of this chapter will look at the effect of taxes on your retirement, including the way your pension can affect your tax bracket. There is one caveat to get out of the way up front, though: These tax brackets and marginal tax rates are for 2015. They are subject to change. We are in a time of historically low tax rates—we haven't seen rates this low since the early twentieth century.

Will these low tax rates remain in place during your retirement? We don't know. They have shifted before and they will probably

2 http://www.usinflationcalculator.com/inflation/current-inflation-rates/

shift again. The federal deficit will exert pressure here. According to David McKnight's thought-provoking book *The Power of Zero*, the United States government spends seventy-six cents of every tax dollar on just four items: Social Security, Medicare, Medicaid, and interest on the national debt. These four items could consume ninety-two cents of every tax dollar by 2020.

Clearly, this is not sustainable. If Congress doesn't act soon, there won't be money to cover basic government services and obligations. If Congress does act, they may consider raising taxes in addition to cutting expenses. We don't know for sure what they will do, but it is reasonable to anticipate possible tax increases in the future. At our training events, we ask participants whether they believe taxes will go up or down. The overwhelming sentiment among participants is that they will go up. This is because, other than inflation, raising taxes appears to be the government's choice for dealing with the national debt.

Future tax rate hikes can have a major effect on your retirement income streams, especially if you have a lot of your money in "tax-me-later" buckets such as a traditional TSP and a traditional IRA instead of an investment account with a Roth "wrapper." If you have been deferring your taxes until later, you may want to consider diversifying in order to limit your future tax liability.

TAXES IN RETIREMENT

Most people have a fairly good grasp of their tax situation while they are working. Although this is definitely a good thing, it can create the illusion that you understand how your taxes will work in retirement. Most federal employees don't realize, or fail to appreciate, how their taxes will change—*or not change as they expect them to*—in retirement.

Paying taxes is rarely simple, but it tends to get even more complex once you retire. You will not stop paying income taxes just because you quit working. In fact, you will have to pay taxes on monies withdrawn from certain retirement accounts.

Most federal retirees also have to pay federal income tax on some of their Social Security benefits. In fact, your tax situation could become more complex during your retirement than it was when you were working, thanks to the way your federal annuity, Social Security benefits, TSP withdrawals, investment income, and wages earned in retirement work together. Consider, for example, the way that drawing from your TSP in retirement can trigger a double tax—one on your savings and a second on your Social Security. (See Chapter 5 for more information on this double tax.)

Most federal retirees expect their tax bracket to be lower upon retirement, but as we shall see in this chapter, that is often not the case. Practically all of your annuity will be subject to federal tax in retirement, creating a radically different tax situation than what your friends in the private sector may experience.

To be clear, your large annuity is a good thing. Be thankful for it! But do understand the tax implications of this asset and employ the asset-maximization strategy that works best for you.

TAX BRACKETS

Let's now look more closely at how your annuity can affect your marginal tax rate in retirement. The taxes chart that appears below summarizes the basic 2015 federal tax structure. Although every case is different, there is a good chance that you, as a federal employee, will not be in as low a tax bracket as you may think. Many people in the 25 and 28 percent brackets believe they will fall down into the 15 percent bracket—a significant decrease in the marginal tax rate. All too often they find that it doesn't work out as planned.

Now you may be thinking: *But wait! Suze Orman, Clark Howard, Dave Ramsey, and countless other TV and radio personalities have told me again and again that I will drop down to a lower tax bracket upon retirement.* This is not always true, especially for federal employees, who receive such robust pensions. The generous benefits that federal employees receive, coupled with the federal tax structure, often keep retirees in the same bracket.

Consider the case of two FERS employees, Crystal and Tim, a married couple, who are both sixty years old. Crystal has an annual salary of $133,000, and Tim makes $83,000 per year. They are currently living well within their means. They both plan to retire in two years at age sixty-two. Crystal expects to receive an annuity of $1,710 per month and another $1,582 from Social Security. Tim will receive a pension of $1,756 per month in retirement and a monthly Social Security check for $1,190.

Their salaries put them near the top of the 25 percent marginal income tax bracket while working. They expect to drop into a lower tax bracket when they retire, because celebrity financial gurus have repeated this ad nauseam on TV and in books. Tim and Crystal have been contributing to their individual TSP accounts rather than a Roth account because they expect lower tax rates on their tax-deferred retirement funds.

What Tim and Crystal don't realize is that their federal pensions will actually keep them in the same marginal tax bracket even after retirement. Marginal tax brackets are generally based upon adjusted gross income (AGI). Their AGI includes 85 percent of their Social Security benefits, since their combined income exceeds specified limits (see Chapter 5 on Social Security for more details on how this works). In their case, their AGI will only fall to $74,900 in retirement, which will cause them to remain in the same 25 percent marginal income tax bracket (based on the taxes chart) even after standard deductions and exemptions. We see this almost all the time with "dual-fed" couples, and it is a common occurrence for single federal retirees as well.

Consult the chart on the following page for a breakdown of the 2015 federal income tax brackets, and to observe how Tim and Crystal shift within their marginal income bracket—but not out of it—when they move into retirement.

Keep in mind that tax brackets are subject to change every year. (Visit our website for the latest numbers.) We expect the dollar ranges for each bracket to continue to go up slowly over time due to inflation adjustments, though this is not a given.

http://retireinstitute.com/your
-benefits/tax-planning/

Status	10%	15%	25%	28%	33%	35%	39.6%
Single	9,225	37,450	90,750	189,300	411,500	413,200	MAX
MFJ	18,450	74,900	151,200	230,450	411,500	464,850	MAX
HoH	13,150	50,200	129,600	209,850	411,500	439,000	MAX

```
                                                              39.6%
                                                     35%
                                                     464,850
                                         33%
                                28%      411,500
                        25%     230,450
                15%     151,200
        10%     74,900
   MFJ  18,450                           * Tax brackets for 2015
```

Knowing what tax bracket you will be in when you retire is important for retirement planning. Having put their savings in "tax-me-later" traditional TSPs, and not dropping to a lower tax bracket, they missed out on the primary advantage of the traditional TSP. Saving money in a tax-deferred account is often a good idea, but as we can see with Tim and Crystal, changing to Roth savings can provide needed diversification.

The couple also believes that tax rates will most likely increase in the future. If this ends up being true, it would be another good reason to contribute to a Roth account.

Please note: We do not know what changes will occur in the future of the tax system. If taxes increase, Tim and Crystal might save real tax dollars by using Roth accounts; if taxes remain the same, they would maintain the same position by funding tax-deferred accounts. There is no crystal ball though, and the future is uncertain. Thus, we like to follow the advice of the wisest and richest man who ever lived. In Ecclesiastes 11:2 (God's Word translation), King Solomon says:

Divide what you have into seven parts, or even into eight,
Because you don't know what disaster may happen on earth.

You plan for uncertainty through diversification. We talk of diversifying our investment structures into stocks, bonds, gold, or real estate ... but what about our tax strategies? These, too, can be diversified.

The takeaway from this chapter: Everyone's financial situation is unique, and the tax system is difficult to navigate successfully. You should be working with a tax professional and financial professional who are knowledgeable about federal benefits in order to minimize the bite that taxes will take out of your retirement savings, both now and later. While it is never too late, planning for the future early will help you optimize your tax efficiency.

DON'T FORGET STATE TAXES!

Depending on where you reside, you may have to pay state income taxes. State income taxes can vary dramatically from state to state. It can be a good retirement strategy to retire in a state that will lower your tax burden.

Retiring in a state with no income tax is a commonsense approach, but it is not always the best strategy. This can be counterintuitive, because you may think that no income tax is always the optimal situation. But consider this: The state government has to collect taxes from *somewhere*. If they aren't filling the state's coffers with income taxes, they are raising revenues through other taxes, usually property taxes and sales taxes. Retirees often pay these taxes.

Some states exclude pension income from taxes entirely, or they may tax only a certain amount of retirement income at a certain age. Because there are so many variations, you will need to consult your own state's rules. Proper planning, just in the arena of state income tax, can save 6 percent or more of your retirement income.

For example, in Georgia, where Retirement Benefits Institute is headquartered, generally the first $35,000 of pension income is excluded from taxation once retirees hit age sixty-two. At age sixty-five, the first $65,000 of pension income is not taxable. Compare that to nearby Florida and Tennessee, which have no income tax, but may have higher sales taxes and property taxes. Why not retire in a state where everyone pays income tax but you?

This is only one example of how to offset your tax liability by choosing a state to retire in strategically. Make sure to build state income tax provisions into your income planning.

CHAPTER 9

Federal Employees Group Life Insurance

NO ONE LIKES thinking about their own passing. If we called this book "death and taxes," no one would pick it up!

There will come a time, however, when we will all pass from this world to the next. It is important to have your affairs—and that includes your financial affairs—in order before that time comes. You need to make sure that you have the life insurance coverage necessary to protect the ones you love.

As a federal employee, you have the option of getting life insurance through the Federal Employees Group Life Insurance (FEGLI) program. FEGLI is group term insurance that has a basic benefit and three add-on options. It can be a great tool, but costs may spiral out of control as you get older. The basic benefit cost doesn't increase as you age, but the options' costs increase every five years—and dramatically so, as you will see.

BASIC FEGLI

The basic FEGLI benefit coverage is derived from your salary. To calculate your basic benefit, take your annual basic pay rounded up to the nearest $1,000 and add $2,000. For example: If Josh, a federal employee, has an annual basic pay of $99,749, he would be eligible for a basic FEGLI coverage amount of $102,000.

Federal employees who are under the age of forty-five may receive some extra basic benefit through an add-on, up to double the basic benefit for employees thirty-five and younger. Consult the OPM website for details.

The basic cost will not automatically increase as you get older, but it will increase as your salary grows, and then again at retirement.

FEGLI OPTIONS WHILE EMPLOYED

There are three options you may choose to add onto your basic FEGLI. You can add any combination of these options, or none at all. However, it is required that you enroll in basic coverage to participate in any of the other FEGLI options.

Option A provides an additional $10,000 of death benefit. This option is typically inexpensive, but it does increase in price every five years.

Option B also provides additional coverage, but rather than a flat amount, the increase in benefit is based on your salary. You can choose any multiple between one and five times your annual salary, effectively raising your benefit by a factor of up to sixfold. If Josh took Option Bx5, his basic benefit of $102,000 would increase by $500,000, giving him $602,000 in coverage.

This is a substantial amount of life insurance for some, but depending on your debt, income, assets, and needs, it may not be enough for you.

Option C provides family coverage, allowing you to obtain life insurance on your spouse and eligible dependent children. This option provides flat-rate coverage that can be purchased in multiples of up to five. Each multiple adds $5,000 of coverage for your spouse and $2,500 for each child. Children may no longer be covered under Option C once they turn eighteen years old, or twenty-two if they attend college.

Option C coverage does not cancel automatically when the person covered is no longer eligible. We often see people paying for Option C when they have no one who would be covered by it. If you no longer have children of an eligible age and/or you are no longer married, update your Option C coverage to reflect these facts. No one wants to pay for nothing!

BUT WHAT DOES IT COST?

Option A is the cheapest FEGLI option, but with a benefit of only $10,000, it is not enough for most people. Generally, the benefit of Option B is higher than that of Option A, but so are the costs. Option B is the most expensive of the FEGLI options, and the cost increases every five years.

Let's look at the cost of FEGLI as you progress through your federal career. We will again return to Josh as an example. Remember, he has a salary of $99,749. Assume that he has opted to take basic FEGLI as well as the Bx5 option. The following chart maps out Josh's FEGLI costs as they increase over the course of his career:

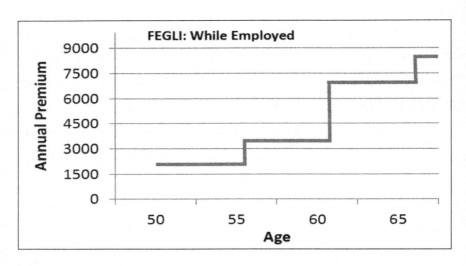

FEGLI PRICE INCREASES

As you can see, FEGLI prices increase every five years, with the most substantial increase occurring at age sixty. In Josh's case, the cost rose 112 percent between the age of fifty-nine and sixty!

The poor cost-benefit ratio for FEGLI Option B can make it prohibitive for some and a bad deal for many. You may have more cost-effective options for getting this much coverage on the private market, which is something you should at least explore.

The drastic increase in FEGLI costs while working is appreciable, but what you may not know is that prices can soar even higher in retirement. Let's now look at how FEGLI works after you retire.

FEGLI IN RETIREMENT

To carry FEGLI into retirement, you must retire on an immediate annuity, be insured on your retirement date, and have been enrolled in FEGLI either for the five years prior to retirement or since your first opportunity to enroll. If these conditions are not met, you are ineligible to carry FEGLI into retirement. Thankfully, FEGLI is not an all-or-nothing proposition. You can choose to keep only a portion of it in retirement. Upon retiring, you will need to decide whether to keep FEGLI, reduce it, or replace it. You'll have different choices for the basic benefit and the three options.

For basic FEGLI, you're given the choice of no reduction in your benefit, a 50 percent reduction, or a 75 percent reduction. The chart below shows the cost of these choices, based on an original death benefit of $100,000. Many people decide to keep the basic benefit with the 75 percent reduction because it becomes free at age sixty-five and provides a minimal benefit for the rest of your life. The 75 percent reduction is a benefit of FEGLI you typically won't find in the private market. (See following page.)

FEGLI BASIC CHOICES AT RETIREMENT			
Choices for Basic:	**Basic Coverage Reduced to:**	**Monthly Premium until Age 65:**	**Monthly Premium after Age 65:**
No Reduction	$100,000	$226	$194
50% Reduction	$50,000	$96	$64
75% Reduction	$25,000	$32	Free

Retirement affects the benefits and costs of the three FEGLI add-on options differently. Option A is very simple. The premiums simply end at age sixty-five, meaning there is no reason to reduce this option if you already have it. However, the benefit will begin reducing by 2 percent per month until it lands at $2,500. This is a no-brainer—if you have it, keep it!

Options B and C both allow you to opt for either a full reduction or no reduction. With the full-reduction choice, premiums stop at age sixty-five and the benefit amount reduces 2 percent per month until it is completely eliminated. If you choose no reduction for these options, you will retain the same coverage amount you had while employed. However, the cost will continue to rise every five years until age eighty, which can get very expensive, especially for Option B.

The next chart, Full FEGLI Benefits into Retirement, illustrates what would happen if Josh, with his salary of $99,749 and basic FEGLI plus option Bx5, carried full benefits into retirement:

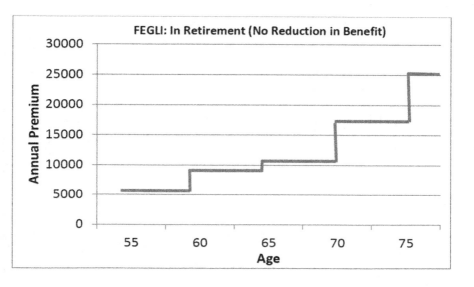

FULL FEGLI BENEFITS INTO RETIREMENT

Josh's FEGLI costs started around $1,400 per year when he was employed at age forty-five. By the time retirement rolls around and he reaches his late seventies, his costs will have increased to approximately $25,000 per year. These numbers may seem astonishing. Who would keep the benefits at such extreme costs?

There are some rare cases in which it may make sense. If you need insurance and cannot get it on the private market, FEGLI may be your best option. For example, we have known retirees who fell sick with a terminal illness for which they could not get private coverage. In such cases, FEGLI would be an option to consider. For the vast majority of federal retirees, however, it may make more sense to look at options beyond FEGLI.

The reason FEGLI becomes prohibitively expensive as you age is that it was designed to do so. FEGLI was never intended to be a long-term solution to your insurance needs. Remember, it is a group term policy.

If your FEGLI benefits aren't going to provide you with the coverage you need, the question you must ask yourself is: *What will?*

SOLUTIONS

The first thing you need to do is determine your actual life insurance needs. There are online tools, such as lifehappens.org, that can give you an estimate of your actual death benefit need. You don't want to be underinsured. You also don't want to be paying for more life insurance than you actually need. This is a common mistake. Consider your individual needs. For example, if you no longer have a mortgage, you may not need as much life insurance to ensure that your spouse can keep the house.

Your other option is to consider private insurance. This gives you the most potential options and control, but you do have to qualify for any coverage you receive. If you are in average to excellent health, private insurance could provide a better cost and benefit structure than FEGLI. Most private life insurance policies do not increase prices for the duration of the contract, a significant improvement over FEGLI's five-year price jumps.

Ultimately, the cost of private insurance will depend on your age, health, and other factors as determined by the insurer. It never hurts to shop the market and find the best solutions for you and your family. Ask your financial advisor or insurance agent to run some quotes. You have nothing to lose by exploring your options.

WHAT SHOULD YOUR LIFE INSURANCE DO FOR YOU?

Although everyone's specific needs are different, there are some basic things that most people want out of life insurance. Below are five basic characteristics we advise people to look for in a policy:

- **Your life insurance should be there when you die,** which is when it is actually needed. Regardless of how long you live, you should make sure that the benefit doesn't end before you die.
- **Your life insurance should maximize your pension.** You cannot look at benefits alone—you have to look at costs, too. Be a wise consumer. Don't let rising costs eat away at your pension. Consider the whole package and run a cost-benefit analysis on your options. You can keep different levels of FEGLI, you can choose a survivor annuity option, and there are many options on the private life insurance market. The right choice for you is one that maximizes your pension. (See Chapter 4 for a detailed discussion of survivor benefits.)
- **Your life insurance has the potential to be a tax-free asset.** It can also be a tax-free vehicle for other assets. If managed properly through advanced

strategies, life insurance policies can build cash value that can be accessed tax-free through retirement.

On top of the potential tax-free living benefits, life insurance that is paid for with after-tax dollars has a tax-free death benefit.

- **Your life insurance should have the potential to provide a long-term care benefit.** If you desire some type of permanent life insurance program, consider one with flexible living benefits. Some allow you to access portions of your death benefit early to provide for chronic illness expenses. This affords you the flexibility to use the same assets to cover your life insurance needs or unexpected health care costs.

- **Your life insurance should provide asset protection.** Assets you hold in the bank, investments, and other property can potentially be accessed by creditors. A car accident makes for a bad day. Lawyers seeking to tap your non-qualified, unprotected assets to gain restitution for an accident you caused during retirement make for an even worse day. Life insurance policies may be exempt from creditors, which could shield a portion of your assets. Check your state laws to see how this works in your area.

If your policy fulfills all or most of these five conditions and is still affordable for you, then it's likely a good policy. Such a policy can help make you financially independent.

Take, for example, the case of George, a federal employee five years from retirement. Upon turning fifty-five, his FEGLI costs increased drastically. This increase drove him to consider his other options. Being so close to retirement, he wanted to incorporate survivor annuity planning for his wife as well.

George knew this was more than he could handle alone. He consulted an insurance professional who understood his federal benefits. Together, they worked out a plan to replace his FEGLI *and* take care of his wife in the event that he passed away first.

The plan had an extra benefit: George bought a permanent policy with a chronic illness rider. This would allow him to use some of his death benefit for long-term-care expenses, if needed, which gave him and his wife peace of mind. The permanent policy also had a cash value component that could grow tax-free.

By enacting this plan, George simplified his life insurance and maximized his future pension. See our video here.

http://retireinstitute.com /resources/videos/

When shopping for a life insurance policy, you have to consider your needs and your overall financial situation. It's more than just buying a policy. It is an integral part of financial planning. You need to do proper analysis and planning before you pick one.

Don't delay evaluating your situation and weighing your options. Pull out your pay stubs and receipts right now and see what you're paying for life insurance and FEGLI benefits. Are you being a wise consumer? Do you know all of your current and future options, or do you need to shop around? Do you understand the costs and benefits of your plan and other plans on the market?

If not, it's time to study up and consult a professional. At Retirement Benefits Institute, we can help you calculate what your FEGLI and survivor annuity costs will be going forward as you create a plan that works for you.

http://retireinstitute.com
/resources/retirement-benefits
-analysis/

Chapter 10

Federal Employees Health Benefits in Retirement, Federal Long-Term Care Insurance Policy, and Medicare

FEDERAL EMPLOYEES AND retirees may participate in the Federal Employees Health Benefits (FEHB) program. The program is an umbrella that encompasses a number of different carriers and plans. Your own situation and health care needs, as well as those of your family, will dictate which plan is best for you. Again, it's all about understanding your options so that you can choose the one that maximizes your benefits while reducing your costs.

In most cases, FEHB remains unchanged as you enter retirement. You will typically have the same coverage options and the same open seasons in retirement that you enjoyed while employed. The federal government even continues to pay the same percentage of health care costs (either 75 percent of the carrier's total premium or 72 percent of the average premium, whichever is less), though you will see normal annual increases. Very few employers other than the federal government still offer this kind of coverage to retirees.

One instance in which your FEHB might change in retirement is if the federal government changes the plan the same year that you retire. Such a coincidence is unlikely, however, and would not actually be triggered by your retirement.

BE READY FOR THE PREMIUM CONVERSION—YOU WILL SWITCH!

Aside from your normal annual increases, the only other additional expense associated with FEHB that you'll see in retirement is the premium conversion that accompanies the switch from paying your premium with pretax dollars to after-tax dollars. While you're employed, FEHB premiums are paid with before-tax dollars. However, in retirement the premiums are paid with after-tax dollars, which may increase your tax bill.

— PLANNING TIP —

The premium conversion opens some opportunities to strategize for couples in which both spouses are federally employed. If one spouse retires before the other, the employed spouse may want to carry coverage for the family under their benefits to take advantage of the before-tax treatment.

For example, consider Sheila and James, a married couple who are both FERS employees. Sheila is planning to retire in 2015. James doesn't plan to retire until 2020. Because he will be working longer, James may find it advantageous to carry a FEHB family plan that covers both him and Sheila. This way, the couple can continue paying premiums with before-tax dollars for as long as James continues working.

FEHB ELIGIBILITY

To keep your FEHB coverage in retirement, you must be enrolled for the five years prior to your retirement. Time spent under TRICARE, which is offered by the Department of Defense, counts toward your five-year requirement for FEHB, but you still must be enrolled in FEHB by the last open-enrollment period before retirement in order to carry FEHB in retirement. Some employees with TRICARE switch to FEHB just before retirement so that they will have the option of TRICARE, FEHB, and/or Medicare in retirement.

You can switch back to TRICARE if you want to after retirement. We recommend that you suspend FEHB at retirement, which you may do and still return to it at a later open-enrollment period. The keyword here is *suspend*. You never want to actually cancel your FEHB coverage because doing so may preclude you from getting it back. You can suspend and re-enroll in FEHB later for any reason if you so choose. We see some federal retirees suspend FEHB to reduce monthly insurance costs.

Your spouse, as well as any children under the age of twenty-six, may also be enrolled in your plan. If your spouse is not federally employed, they may still be eligible for spousal continuance upon your passing if you were enrolled in the FEHB Family Plan at the time of your death and also selected the survivor's benefit option discussed in Chapter 4. Any special-needs children are eligible to remain on your FEHB coverage upon your passing if they are listed as survivor annuitants.

MEDICARE

Federal employees become eligible for Medicare coverage at age sixty-five just like everyone else. At this point, you will have some important decisions to make regarding your future health care needs. Before looking at how Medicare and FEHB interact, let us first examine Medicare itself.

Medicare is a complicated program. The following discussion is only intended to provide you with a basic framework for decision making. For a full explanation of choices and programs, please review medicare.gov and consult a professional.

Medicare has several parts that address different health care needs. **Medicare Part A** is hospital insurance that generally covers inpatient care in hospitals, skilled nursing facilities, hospice, and home health care. You will not have to pay premiums for Medicare Part A, provided that you paid Medicare taxes while working. This is typically the case for federal retirees because both CSRS and FERS employees pay Medicare taxes.

Medicare Part B is the most discussed part of the Medicare programs, as well as the most utilized. Part B generally covers doctors' services, outpatient care, home health services, other medical services, and some preventive services. In 2015, the average monthly cost of Part B premiums was $104.90.

There is a seven-month window in which you can enroll in Medicare Part B coverage without facing penalties. If you wish to avoid these penalties, you must enroll within the three months prior to the month you turn sixty-five, the month of your sixty-fifth birthday itself, or the three months after your birthday month. This window applies only if you choose to retire at any age before sixty-five; if you are still working and covered under FEHB when you reach age sixty-five, you may wait until you retire to enroll and not be subjected to any penalties, provided you enroll within eight months of retiring.

If you decide not to enroll in Medicare within the defined windows and later decide to enroll, you will then be subject to penalties. The late enrollment penalty is 10 percent of the Part B premiums for each twelve-month period you were eligible to enroll but did not. As you can see, this penalty can get costly if you realize you should have enrolled in Part B several years late. This doesn't mean that Medicare is right for everyone, but it does mean that you should look at all of your options and make an informed decision when you retire. Failing to do so could cost you considerably.

Medicare Part C, also known as Medicare Advantage, is not actually a government program. Medicare Advantage is coverage offered by private companies that have been approved by Medicare.

Medicare Part D is prescription drug coverage. These plans are either run by an insurance company or by a private company approved by Medicare. You may not enroll in Medicare Part D alone. You either have to add Part D to your other Medicare options or enroll in a Medicare Advantage plan and receive all Medicare coverage through the plan.

FEHB AND MEDICARE PART B

One of the most common questions federal employees ask us at Retirement Benefit Institute is: "Should I enroll in Medicare?"

There is no one correct answer to this question. What's best for you depends on many factors, but we can share with you what we commonly see retirees selecting and why they make these choices.

The majority of people enroll in Part A because they have already paid for it, so the biggest question is: "Should I enroll in Part B?"

As a federal employee with FEHB, the three most common options when it comes to Medicare Part B are:

- **Do not enroll in Part B. Keep FEHB in place as your primary coverage.**
- **Enroll in Part B. Suspend FEHB.**
- **Enroll in Part B. Keep FEHB in place as your secondary coverage.**

OPTION 1: Do Not Enroll in Part B and Keep FEHB as Your Primary Coverage

In some situations, federal employees might choose not to enroll in Medicare Part B and just keep their FEHB coverage. They may want to ensure that their FEHB remains their primary coverage. These days, many doctors no longer accept Medicare patients. If your doctors don't accept Medicare, this may preclude you from seeing them. If this matters to you or if you don't want to potentially limit your choices, you may decide to keep FEHB and not to enroll in Medicare.

OPTION 2: Enroll in Part B and Suspend FEHB

If you want to enroll in Part B but don't want to continue paying for FEHB, you can suspend FEHB. Notice that we used the word *suspend* again for FEHB—do not cancel! Suspending FEHB will allow you to return to FEHB if you later decide that you would like to have both Part B and FEHB. You can re-enroll in FEHB during a future open-enrollment period. Suspending FEHB may result in lower monthly premiums. For some people, this may make the most sense, but be careful, as some people may receive less benefit this way than by choosing an option that includes keeping FEHB.

If you do elect to suspend FEHB, you may also want to pick up a supplemental plan, such as one of those offered under Medicare Advantage (Part C). With Medicare Advantage, you can get Parts A, B, and D, and you may even add additional coverage, such as dental, vision, and hearing. There are many different Advantage plans from which to choose. Some come with lower premiums and higher out-of-pocket costs, while others have higher premiums but provide better coverage.

OPTION 3: Enroll in Medicare Part B and Keep FEHB in Place

Many federal employees, especially those with health problems or high medical costs, elect to keep dual coverage. If you choose this option, you will need to look at your FEHB plan brochure to see how your particular plan works with Medicare. Your FEHB will always be secondary to Medicare if you keep both benefits into retirement. Be sure to find out which doctors will accept you with Medicare as your primary coverage.

Keeping both FEHB and Medicare will affect your costs. This strategy will result in the highest monthly premiums, since you are paying for both programs, but typically you will have the lowest out-of-pocket costs for medical needs. That trade-off may or may not be advantageous, depending on your situation. Understand the costs you are likely to face and decide carefully.

No matter which of the three options you choose, you should first seek professional advice. We are painting in broad strokes here—Medicare is a complex set of programs!

THE FEDERAL LONG-TERM CARE INSURANCE PROGRAM

The Federal Long-Term Care Insurance Program (FLTCIP) provides coverage that will help pay for long-term care (LTC) expenses. This program can significantly defray the costs of home care, assisted-living centers, and nursing homes—all of which can be prohibitively expensive for many people without coverage. The FLTCIP can help provide care for ongoing illnesses or disabilities that prevent you from performing activities of daily living, such as bathing, dressing, eating, transferring, continence, and toileting. These may not be things you think about now, but they may be in the future. See ltcfeds.com for a full discussion of qualifications.

Most federal employees and retirees eligible for FEHB and their qualified relatives can apply for insurance coverage under the FLTCIP. You only have to be eligible for FEHB, not necessarily enrolled, to apply for this LTC coverage. However, eligibility is based on a number of factors and certain medical conditions can disqualify you from FLTCIP coverage.

Premiums for the FLTCIP vary based on your age when you apply and are subject to future increases.

The fine print on these FLTCIP plans can be misleading, however, especially regarding price. For example, some plans are guaranteed never to go up in price ... *unless* the price is raised for everyone, which can happen. In our experience, most LTC programs do end up raising prices over time, as costs are likely to go up eventually. You can also buy LTC coverage on the private market, but if the price for the FLTCIP goes up, it is likely that the same will happen for private LTC.

Don't let the possibility of price increases prevent you from getting the coverage you need, but do know *exactly* what you are getting into when choosing any kind of LTC insurance.

— PLANNING TIP —

Consider your whole financial plan before you buy into the FLTCIP or any other long-term care coverage. You may not need an insurance policy to cover the full cost of LTC. Many people already have "built-in" protections that can reduce this financial burden. Regardless of your health, your federal annuity and Social Security checks will still be there. Your assets, such as your TSP, are yours. If you've paid off your house, you have that as well. Factoring these assets into your retirement plan can be reasonable, thus reducing the amount of LTC needed. Also, certain kinds of life insurance may cover chronic illness needs. Bottom line: Careful planning may shrink your projected LTC insurance needs substantially. Don't buy more coverage than you need.

The refrain of this chapter has been to find a professional who can help you make sense of your health care options. You may want to include your doctors, financial advisors, tax professionals, and a professional who understands federal retirement benefits in this discussion.

You need to start developing a plan now to ensure that you have the coverage you need later. The choices you make at retirement may affect your future health care options and costs. There are many factors to consider when making these kinds of major health care decisions. Will your doctor accept your insurance? Are you willing to switch doctors if he does not? How is your health? What health problems do you face, and how likely is your health to change in the future?

These are questions you may not know the answers to until you are close to decision time. You can never truly know what the future will bring in regard to your health. There are other unknowns as well, such as how the Affordable Care Act and any future reforms to health care coverage will change the face of Medicare and FEHB. Again, because there is such uncertainty surrounding your health and the future of health care, we highly recommend talking to a professional who can help you understand your options so that you can make informed choices with confidence.

CHAPTER 11

Budgeting in Retirement

A SPECIAL THANKS to my dear friend and partner Mark Wilson who not only helped develop the content of this book, but wrote the majority of this chapter.

Much of this book has been dedicated to helping you understand the ins and outs of your retirement income as a federal retiree. Income is only half of the retirement planning equation, though. Just as important as the money coming in is the money going out. Budgeting is an important part of retirement planning. Just as you need a plan for bringing in retirement funds, you also need a strategy for the spending of those funds.

When drawing up a retirement budget, first ask yourself: *What will I need to live on in retirement?*

Budgeting is not something most people would describe as fun. The average person is more likely to deem budgeting as "the B word," something best not thought about! However, budgeting is crucial to sound retirement planning. You should create a retirement budget while you are still working so that you can get your expenses under control *before* you retire. Also, some choices about retirement must be made before you reach retirement age. Delaying planning could close off options that you might have otherwise had.

Start planning a retirement budget by examining how you currently spend your money. Build out a basic framework for your budget that includes household expenses, auto expenses, groceries, dining out, clothing, and gifts (for example, birthdays and Christmas). Don't forget the little things. We recommend reviewing six to twelve months of previous spending to determine where your money has actually gone. There is a tendency to underestimate what we spend on discretionary purchases, be they in the form of nice dinners out, expensive treats, or those extra gifts for the grandchildren.

The next step is to calculate your retirement income. A professional can help you come up with an accurate estimate.

Once you have an estimate of your retirement income and a comprehensive budget that takes into account all of your current expenses, you can begin to formulate a retirement budget. An accurate current budget can serve as a template for your retirement budget, and this will allow you to see exactly what will have to change. To start drafting your retirement budget, begin identifying areas in your current budget that will increase, decrease, or altogether disappear in retirement.

Maybe some expenses will be reduced, such as gas and clothing now that you no longer have to commute or purchase office attire. Some payments may continue, such as health insurance premiums, home insurance, and cell phone bills. Some expenses may or may not continue into retirement, such as mortgage payments and car payments. For many people, one of the biggest reductions in monthly expenses is that you will no longer have to make contributions to retirement accounts. Retirement marks your exit from the accumulation phase and entrance into the distribution phase of life.

Other expenses may increase, such as travel and spoiling the grandchildren. Again, pay special attention to discretionary spending. Are you really willing to give up dinners out and organic produce? If not, they had better be in your retirement budget.

After drafting a retirement budget, you'll have a much better idea of what to expect in retirement. You will also be able to formulate a realistic plan for getting to where you want to be. Some people find that it's best to delay retirement until certain expenses are taken off the budget, such as a mortgage or car payment. Some potential retirees may put off retirement until their children are out of college, employed, and self-sufficient.

THREE TIPS FOR CREATING A SUCCESSFUL RETIREMENT BUDGET

There are three tips Retirement Benefits Institute recommends everyone heed when creating the ever-so-important retirement budget:

1. **Consider whether your house and car fit into your long-term plans.** Some people decide they do not want such a big house in retirement now that the children are gone and have families of their own. Many retirees decide not to own a home at all in retirement, but to rent instead. This reduces the stress of keeping up a home in retirement. Likewise, you probably won't need that large SUV anymore if it's just you and your spouse going on road trips together. Why pay *for what you don't really want or need?*

2. **Plan for non-monthly expenses.** Do not forget to include all expenses in your budget, whether they occur monthly or not. Birthdays and Christmas come but once a year, but the expense is regular. Don't forget car registration and repair costs. Include any annual vacations. Include everything. It may help you to divide regular non-monthly payments down to their monthly costs. So, for example, if you spend $3,000 a year on a summer vacation, block that out as $250 a month.

3. **Get the whole family involved.** When drafting your budget, the most important family member to include is, of course, your spouse. Financial pressures are one of the largest drivers of marital conflict. Although including your spouse in all aspects of your retirement planning may be an unpleasant process at first, it's of paramount importance that you and your partner are on the same page. Even if you are the one monitoring and planning finances alone, your spouse can help keep you accountable and on track—but only if he or she is kept informed.

— PLANNING TIP —

If you are single, we encourage you to find an account-ability partner whom you can trust to tell you the straight truth and help hold you accountable.

These tips and strategies can help you put together a retirement budget that's accurate and comprehensive. Managing expenses and cash outflow is just as important as planning your retirement income. Don't delay the planning process, and don't hesitate to see a professional who can help you plan for the future.

The sample budget sheet we've included on the following page can help you to begin the process. This worksheet is also available on our website at retireinstitute.com:

Monthly Budget

Monthly Income

Bring Home $ -
Salary _____
Interest _____
Dividends _____
Other Income _____
1. Less $ -
Tithe/Giving (10%) _____
Taxes _____
Net Spendable Income $ -

Monthly Living Expenses

2. Housing $ -
Mortgage/Rent _____
Insurance _____
Property Taxes _____
Electricity _____
Gas _____
Water _____
Sanitation _____
Telephone _____
Maintenance _____
Cable TV _____
Home Services _____
Lawn & Garden _____
Other _____
3. Transportation $ -
Payments _____
Gas & Oil _____
Insurance _____
License/Taxes _____
Maint./Repair _____
Other _____
4. Insurance $ -
Life _____
Health _____
Other _____
5. Medical $ -
Doctor _____
Dentist _____
Prescriptions _____
Other _____

6. Food/Household $ -
Groceries/Household _____
Dining Out _____
7. Financial Management $ -
Debts _____
Investments _____
Savings _____
Other _____
8. Entertainment/Recreation $ -
Movies/Books/Music _____
Activities/Trips _____
Vacation _____
Pets _____
Memberships _____
Other _____
9. Miscellaneous $ -
Clothing _____
Beauty/Barber _____
Gifts (incl. Christmas) _____
Cell Phone _____
Subscriptions _____
Allowances _____
Cash _____
Other _____
10. School/Child Care $ -
Child Support _____
Baby-sitters _____
Materials _____
Transportation _____
Day Care _____
Tuition _____
11. Margin of Error _____

Total Living Expenses $ -

Income vs. Living Expenses

Net Spendable Income $ -

Less Total Living Expenses $ -

Surplus or Deficit $ -

CHAPTER 12

Your Final Destination:
Financial Freedom in Retirement

IN ADDITION TO working hard and saving diligently, navigating the path to financial freedom in retirement requires a good map and a trusted navigator. The map is your retirement plan. The navigator is a professional who can help you draw the map and stay the course.

We encourage federal employees on the way to retirement to occasionally pause and make sure they are charting the correct course. Before you can be confident that you are on the right path, you should be able to affirm seven retirement-readiness statements on the following page:

THE SEVEN RETIREMENT-READINESS STATEMENTS

1. I have accurately calculated my service history for retirement purposes.

2. I have considered my survivor benefits and life insurance options and have chosen the best route to ensure my pension for my spouse or family member(s).

3. I understand the factors that must be considered in order to maximize my Social Security benefit.

4. I know how to leverage my Thrift Savings Plan and other investments effectively in retirement.

5. I have a plan to minimize the impact of taxes and inflation throughout retirement.

6. I am aware of the FEGLI cost structure, both as an employee and as a retiree.

7. I am confident that my income will meet my long-term retirement needs.

Do these seven statements accurately describe you? If so, you are most likely headed toward true financial freedom.

Do not panic if you cannot affirm some of these statements, or even all of them. You still have time to reach out and get the help you need. We implore you to meet with a professional who can guide you to retirement readiness.

TRUE FINANCIAL FREEDOM IS WITHIN YOUR REACH

So you have drawn up your map. You have had a "navigator" verify the plan and guide you down the path. What now? Your final destination: true financial freedom, a place where all of your retirement dreams can become reality.

We could spend all day talking about the benefits of retirement readiness, but nothing is more powerful than the testimony of someone who has been there. Take a moment to read the story of one federal retiree who made a commitment to planning for her future and reaped the rewards of doing so.

My husband and I have two sons. My plan for working—or rather, retiring—was to turn in my keys once both boys were out of college. Looking back now, I wonder—what was I thinking? We had been putting away savings in a college fund since before the boys were even born. They had even both received generous scholarships. Nevertheless, we were having trouble making the numbers work. I found myself having to work past my eligibility age and years of service.

Then I attended a retirement seminar held at my agency. As a human resources officer, I attended in order to be better informed when discussing retirement with my staff. I never dreamed that I would find the seminar as useful personally as I did. The people running the seminar offered to do a personal analysis of my own retirement numbers. This would give me an estimate of my bring-home pay in retirement. I completed a simple budget, provided payroll information and other necessary documents, and waited to see what my retirement estimate would be.

(Please note, this situation does not happen for everyone. I was a CSRS employee with many years of service, but you may find that you are in a similar boat once you run your own numbers.)

I could clearly see that my retirement date would be much sooner than I had planned. I would not be working until my boys got out of college after all!

It was soon to be my time. I had been told by a good friend that I would "just know" when the time was right to retire. They were right! I did just know, but I also had my annuity estimate in writing as proof! I retired on 12/31/2011. Walking out the door of my agency, I sang, "Free at last! Free at last!" all the way to the car.

So what did I do next? I started implementing the retirement plan I had made for myself.

Since I dropped money into the Voluntary Contribution Program [Note: This is discussed in Chapter 7 of this book], *I was able to then withdraw it and roll it into a Roth IRA. Thanks to the same people who had run the seminar, I knew I could contribute up to 10 percent of my federal lifetime earnings, and I took full advantage of this one-time deal. I consider myself a conservative investor. Some of the money went into a fixed indexed annuity and some went into mutual funds at managed risk.*

My husband is also a federal employee and is still working. I chose to leave no survivor annuity for him if I pass away. Yes, he had to agree and sign off on my retirement paperwork, and it had to be witnessed by a notary. I also re-evaluated my life insurance program to ensure that he and my sons will be covered when I die.

Having happily made all of the required retirement decisions, I stepped into retirement and have never looked back.

Now for the good part: Let me tell you about the freedom you can look forward to once you are retired. You will no longer need a clock or watch. I actually took a ten-day vacation and drove to my hometown in another state without even taking a watch. I spent quality time with relatives and friends without being bothered with time constraints. I also did not have to worry about leaving to get back home in order to be back at work.

Travel has been a passion of mine. My husband helped me celebrate my retirement with a cruise to Spain, Italy, and France. We visit Virginia Beach, Memphis, and Atlanta whenever we can get away. I also travel with several groups of friends and relatives on an annual basis. Two of these groups are human resources friends from around the U.S. with whom I worked during my career. Sisters, cousins, and friends love to travel together, and we have met at Branson, Missouri, and taken several cruises. I truly hate to turn down an opportunity to have fun. Life is good. In fact, life has never been better!

Oh, the fun you can have when you actually have the time! Cooking, reading, movies, gardening, lunches, dinners, cleaning closets, donating clothes and shoes that have accumulated for years, exercising, attending family events etc... the possibilities are endless, and I explore new ones each day.

I try to make every day count. I get up in the morning and do the happy dance all the way to the kitchen. I stir up a little breakfast, make my coffee, and sit down and watch the Today Show *and read the newspaper. I rarely had the chance to do that during my working years. I can now sleep past 5:00 a.m. All of this time has allowed me to make daily progress on a bucket list. Not only am I always marking things off the list—I am also adding new things to look forward to in the days to come.*

My workaholic days are over. I no longer need to take blood pressure medicine! Stress is a thing of the past. There are no bad days in retirement. This is the result of my hard work, good retirement planning, and positive attitude. It has been said that everyone chooses their attitude, and I choose to keep on the happy side every day. Retirement is permanent vacation, so why shouldn't I be happy? I think retirement is like having six Saturdays and a Sunday, and then starting all over again. What's not to like?

I am truly happy. May all of you be just as happy when you step into retirement.

We have shared this story because we couldn't provide a more stunning description of the kind of retirement you can have when you are truly ready.

Through our seminars, we have met thousands of federal retirees who are either on the path to financial freedom or have already arrived there. We gave them the tools that allowed more educated decisions as they prepared for retirement. This enabled them to make minor corrections that got them back on the track to reaching their dreams and finding true happiness in retirement. It has been a blessing to navigate the retirement pathway with them, and we want only the same for you.

If you are a federal employee headed toward retirement and you cannot fully affirm all seven of the Retirement Readiness Statements, or if you have not had a professional examine your retirement road map, we encourage you to reach out to us at Retirement Benefits Institute so that we can help get you on track. Visit us online at retireinstitute.com. Attend one of our training seminars on federal benefits (you can also request a training event in your area, if there isn't one already). Let us run your numbers for you. Know where you stand so you can explore your options. Let us see how we can help you reach financial freedom and the retirement you want.

A PERSONAL NOTE FROM THE AUTHOR

I have one last bit of guidance to offer you as you navigate your path toward retirement. Along the path of life, we all share one thing in common: We want peace as we travel and peace in knowing where we're going to end up. Personally, I have found that peace in a relationship with Jesus Christ. While it is not my intention to offend anyone, I am passionate about this subject and would like to share my definition of true freedom.

In John 14:6, Jesus said, "I am the way, the truth, and the life, and no man comes to the Father but by me."

While there are many ways to succeed in this world, there is but one that leads to true peace and joy, and ultimately to a wonderful heaven that God has created for you and me. The one thing that keeps us from peace along this journey is sin. As defined in the Bible, sin refers to breaking God's commandments. All of us have sinned against our Maker at some point; we were all born imperfect humans. What we need is someone to take away our sins. Because Jesus was the only one to have never sinned, His blood has the power to make the sinner clean. Because Jesus died on the cross, His blood can wash away our sin, giving us a new life with Him.

John 1:12 reads, "But as many as received Him, to them He gave the power to become the children of God, even to them that believe on His name."

When we receive Jesus as our Lord and Savior, He gives us peace and makes a promise that He will lead us down the paths of righteousness to ultimately have and enjoy the peace that we can only have through a relationship with the God of the Universe.

It is my hope that this book has pointed you toward some financial peace. At this point, you must now consider spiritual peace. If you find yourself still unsure of the path ahead, I would encourage you to turn to Jesus. I encourage you to pick up the Bible and read it. It contains words of life that can bring great peace to anyone who partakes of it. The Bible is the ultimate road map that will lead you to God and bring great clarity to every area of this life.

CPSIA information can be obtained at www.ICGtesting.com
Printed in the USA
BVOW06s2225180316

440939BV00026B/231/P